SCOTLAND'S FIRST WORLD WAR

When you and I are buried
With grasses over head,
The memory of our fights will stand
Above this bare and tortured land,
We knew ere we were dead.

Though grasses grow on Vimy,
And poppies at Messines,
And in High Wood the children play,
The craters and the graves will stay
To show what things have been.

EWART ALAN MACKINTOSH,
GHOSTS OF WAR

Scotland's First World War

KEVIN MUNRO

HISTORIC SCOTLAND
Edinburgh 2014

Published by Historic Scotland
Longmore House · Salisbury Place
Edinburgh EH9 1SH

Kevin Munro asserts the moral rights to be identified as the author of this work

ISBN 978 1 84917 151 9

Front cover: Glenelg War Memorial
© Spencer Woodcock

Frontispiece: Detail from Cecil King *Dazzled Ships at Leith*, Imperial War Museum, London

Back cover: The 4 inch QF gun on Hirta, St Kilda, RCAHMS

Designed and typeset in Sweet Sans by Dalrymple
Printed on Condat Matt 150gsm and bound by Butler Tanner & Dennis, Frome

www.historic-scotland.gov.uk

If you have enjoyed this book, you may like *Scotland's Sporting Buildings* and *Scotland's Canals*, which will be available in autumn 2014. Both titles are published by Historic Scotland.

A great many people have contributed to the research for this book, for which the author is extremely grateful. In particular, he would like to acknowledge the contribution of Dr Gordon Barclay and Allan Kilpatrick of the Royal Commission on the Ancient and Historical Monuments of Scotland. Much of this publication is based on an audit of sites relating to the First World War in Scotland, which was commissioned by Historic Scotland and the Royal Commission on the Ancient and Historical Monuments of Scotland, and undertaken by Dr Barclay.

Many colleagues at Historic Scotland have been involved in this project but special thanks must go to Olwyn Owen and Rachel Pickering for their assistance, encouragement and support, and to Elizabeth McCrone and Devon DeCelles for much helpful advice. The picture research was undertaken by Rachel Pickering, with help from Michelle Andersson, and the original photography was taken by Duncan Peet.

A number of other people have also contributed to this book: John Atkinson and Gillian McSwan (GUARD Archaeology Ltd); Adrienne Breingan and Maggie Wilson (National Museums Scotland); Ian Lowes; Derek Robertson; Trevor Royle; and The Turnberry Resort. Finally, thanks must go to Sydni Canada for her support and patience throughout the project, without which it would not have been possible.

KM

C
PROPERTY OF THE
MINISTRY OF MUNITIONS
PROPERTY OF THE
MINISTRY OF MUNITIONS
M.3

Preface

The First World War touched Scotland in many different ways. Although the Scottish land mass was not attacked in any appreciable way it was impossible to ignore the fact that Scotland became a country at war in 1914.The rush to join the armed forces produced a steady flow of Scottish recruits as young men answered the call for volunteers, mainly for service in Scotland's ten infantry regiments which expanded rapidly with the creation of war service battalions. At the end of July the warships of the Grand Fleet arrived at their war station at Scapa Flow in Orkney following the annual summer manoeuvres and were later joined in the Firth of Forth by the powerful Battle Cruiser Fleet. At the same time the Highlands west and north of the Great Glen became a restricted area to safeguard the northern naval bases and coastal defences and were closed to anyone without the relevant permit.

The war had an immediate impact on the Clydeside shipyards where ninety per cent of Scotland's shipbuilding capacity was concentrated and where the bulk of Britain's warships were built. Due to the demands of the naval war the Clydeside yards entered a profitable period with a total of 481 warships aggregating almost 760,000 tons being constructed between 1914 and 1918. In the steel-working industry, in 1914 Scotland produced 1.2 million tons of steel, around a quarter of the British total, and the demand for munitions meant that the Scottish figure had doubled by 1918 with 24,000 men in full employment in the Clyde valley. Coal underpinned everything and although the stocks of the west of Scotland fields were gradually being diminished they still accounted for 25.5 million tons or roughly ten per cent of the British output.

Scottish women found that they had a role to play in the war effort and one statistic sums up their contribution. The population census of 1911 showed that 185,442 men were employed in the heavy industries of Clydeside but apart from the 2,062 women employed in the Singer Sewing Machine Factory at Clydebank only 3,758 women worked in the heavy sector, most of them in the chemical industry. Five years later, the number of women involved in Scotland's heavy industries had climbed to 18,500 and by 1918 31,500 women were working in the munitions industry in Scotland.

The greatest impact, though was manpower: by the end of the war, the number of Scots in the armed forces amounted to 688,416, consisting of 71,707 in the Royal Navy, 584,098 in the Army and 32,611 in the Royal Flying Corps and Royal Air Force. But that service brought a bitter legacy: the most recent research shows that the Scottish casualty list was over 148,000. One regiment alone, The Royal Scots, lost 11,213 killed in action, most of them from Edinburgh and the east of Scotland. In Glasgow 18,000 young men, or one in fifty-seven of the city's population, did not come back from the war while Dundee's death toll was 4,213 out of a population of 180,000. As the novelist Ian Hay pointed out when the Scottish National War Memorial was opened in Edinburgh Castle in 1928 'big England's sorrow is national, little Scotland's is personal.' This much needed research into the heritage of the First World War shows that very few Scots were left untouched by a war that was supposed to end war.

Trevor Royle
Edinburgh, Spring 2014

BOMB MAKING FOR HOUSEWIVES
Glasgow City Council, licensor SCRAN

Women turning shell casings in the Mons Shell Factory at the Atlas Works of the North British Locomotive Company, Springburn, Glasgow. The factory was one of two new buildings owned by the company, which became dedicated to the production of war materials. From April 1916 until the end of the First World War the factory was used for the production of artillery shells and staffed mainly by women. The average workforce at Mons Factory comprised, on average, 800 female and 275 male employees.

Introduction

STRONG MEN AT STROMNESS
Orkney Islands Council, Licensor SCRAN

Men from the Orkney Royal Garrison Artillery working on the construction of Ness Battery, outside Stromness in Orkney. The battery was part of the defences of the western approach to the harbour at Scapa Flow. The construction of the Ness Battery in 1914–15 was just one tiny piece of an enormous effort in industry, building and military activity undertaken across Scotland, all directed toward a single purpose: the First World War.

The remote community of Glenelg, overlooking the Kylerhea River and the Isle of Skye in north-west Scotland, has a number of highly visible signs of its history. A few miles to the south-east stand Dun Troddan and Dun Telve, two of the uniquely Scottish stone towers known as brochs. Just to the north of the little village stands the ruins of Bernera Barracks, built in the early 1700s in response to the Jacobite Risings of the early years of the century, and the main road leading to the village follows the route of the old military road in the area. And next to the shore in the heart of the village stands the memorial built to commemorate the sixteen men from the community who were killed in the First World War. Undoubtedly one of the most elaborate war memorials in the country, the Glenelg Memorial was paid for by Lady Scott, the local estate owner (front cover). In the years after the war, she offered to pay for either a war memorial or a new pier for the village. Although a new pier was badly needed at the time, the community chose the memorial. Designed by Sir Robert Lorimer, also the architect of the Scottish National War Memorial, it comprises a high stone plinth with a bronze sculpture by Louis Reid Deuchars. Attached to the plinth are the bronze panels listing the names of the dead men, among them Captain George Henry Hall Scott, Lady Scott's own son. Although their memorial is far grander than many others, the experience of the Glenelg community and the impact the war had upon them reflects many similar experiences across Scotland.

For many people today, awareness of the First World War may come from a silent, sombre crowd gathered at the local war memorial on Remembrance Sunday. Alternatively, some may see graves and memorials on a visit to the now silent battlefields and graveyards of France and Belgium. From these encounters only a fraction of the nature and extent of the momentous events will be understood. Scottish soldiers served on almost every major front of the war from the deserts of Palestine and the Near East, through the beaches of Gallipoli, to the towering peaks of the Alps.

CAOLAS-NA-CON
RCAHMS

Painting of a prisoner of war camp at Caolas-na-Con near Kinlochleven in Argyll and Bute. The camp was built to accommodate German prisoners of war who were used to build the road along the southern side of Loch Leven.

Sailors from Scotland patrolled the seas around the globe with the Royal Navy. Civilian shipping braved the dangers of enemy submarines to carry vital supplies. In the skies over the country, aircraft became a new weapon of war, both for attack and defence. Women across Scotland set to work in industries large and small, while others served as nurses and doctors both at home and abroad. Captured enemy soldiers would live and work adjacent to raw recruits in training in fields and factories over the country.

The unprecedented scale of the First World War leaves an enormous historical legacy. The war records of individual units have been preserved and official histories appeared within two years of the end of the war. Twenty-eight volumes of the history of the Great War based on official documents (1923–1949) were written by a number of authors to account for military, naval, air and medical aspects of the conflict while other national histories are also in print. Much visual imagery of the war and its participants exists in photographs, film, paintings and drawings. There are also detailed contemporary maps of the battlefields. However, millions of letters and diaries tell a more personal story, sometimes light-hearted, other times graphic and painful to recall. Historians have collected the recollections of many thousands of the witnesses to the war in recent decades. In addition to the historical documentation, a substantial physical legacy survives in Scotland and other countries. The best-known examples are the vast cemeteries on the former battlefields of Flanders, the Somme and Verdun. Thousands of war memorials in Scotland and around the world each year become the focus for commemoration. Evidence of the impact of the war can be found across Scotland. Much of its heritage has been neglected, vandalised or demolished since 1918. Places and artefacts that do survive lose their associations with the war over time and are slowly being reclaimed by nature. As a result of a detailed research project into the physical legacy of the war recently conducted by Dr Gordon Barclay for Historic Scotland and the Royal Commission on the Ancient and Historical Monuments of Scotland (RCAHMS) the aim of this book is to highlight some of that heritage. There may be many sites across Scotland whose part in the First World War is yet to be realised. But by introducing aspects of specifically Scottish experiences of the war that may have passed generally unnoticed it is hoped that this will generate a wider interest and appreciation of features in the Scottish landscape that would otherwise be overlooked. It is also worth noting that any aspect of the war in Scotland could easily be discussed in far more length than this book provides, but hopefully this book will provide a route to the reader through which those topics in which they are interested can be further explored. A century on, the physical remains of the conflict serve as a testament to the effort of those involved on all sides: to their heroism, suffering, idealism, desperation and sacrifice.

Now that the men and women involved in the First World War are dead, the physical remains in the landscape become even more significant. The last Scottish veteran of the conflict, Alfred Anderson, died in 2005. Claude Choules, who witnessed the German fleet sink in Scapa Flow in 1919, was the last known surviving combatant when he died in 2010. And with the death in 2012 of England's Florence Green, who worked as a nurse towards the end of the conflict, the last veteran of the First World War passed away. While the people involved may be gone, many of the places where they lived, worked, fought, were entertained and amused and also suffered and died, remain. We repay some of that sacrifice with our curiosity, understanding, care and respect for the places where our forebears played their part; these places survive to remind future generations of the efforts and sacrifices their ancestors made at home and abroad.

P.O.W. Camp
Caolas-na-con
1918

The Threat from the Sea

REMOTE DEFENCES
RCAHMS

The 4 inch Quick-Firing gun, located on the eastern side of Village Bay, on the island Of Hirta, St Kilda. This single gun was built following an attack on 15 May 1918 by the German U-boat U90. Its target was the naval signal station on the island. The submarine fired around seventy shells at the tiny island and destroyed its target. Construction was subsequently begun on the gun emplacement, although it did not become operational until October 1918, only a month before the Armistice brought the fighting to an end.

The greatest threat to the United Kingdom in the First World War was from the sea. As an island, Britain had natural defences against the advance of a land army. However there were imminent dangers posed by seaborne invasion, bombardment and naval blockade. For many centuries the strength of the Royal Navy was vital to homeland defence. By contrast, since its unification in 1871 Germany had built a powerful fleet of state-of-the-art warships and by 1914 was one of very few nations on earth capable of opposing and perhaps defeating the British. The offensive power of Germany was not only a danger to the ships of the British fleet, but also to the coastline and harbours, as demonstrated by a bombardment of the towns of Hartlepool and Scarborough on the Yorkshire coast in December 1914. Prior to the outbreak of hostilities, the Royal Navy and most of the population believed that British warships would be sufficient national defence. But it was clear that the fleet required safe harbours where ships could be re-armed and repaired and where crews could rest and recuperate. Other strategic assets would also need protection. A programme of construction began in earnest in 1913 to create a network of coast defences to protect military, industrial and civilian sites.

At the start of war Scotland had fewer existing defences for its ports than southern England as Scotland was considered to be further from naval aggression than those in the south. The largest defended anchorage in Scotland was at Rosyth on the Firth of Forth, adjacent to the monumental Forth Bridge. Rosyth had already been an important defended anchorage since the 1860s but in 1903 new construction started there when the fear of a German challenge to British supremacy in the North Sea grew more acute. At least six strong modern coast artillery batteries were already in place around the Forth when building at the base began. Other modern coast batteries were built at Dundee, Aberdeen and on the Clyde in the first decade of the twentieth century. But with the outbreak of hostilities it was obvious that far more defensive

COAST ARTILLERY BATTERIES
Contains Ordnance Survey Data

A map showing the coast artillery batteries in use during the First World War. The highest concentration of batteries was around the Firth of Forth and Scapa Flow, the two main bases of the Royal Navy in Scotland.

NESS BATTERY
Historic Scotland, Edinburgh

Part of the remains of the coast artillery battery at Ness, Orkney. This site, overlooking Hoy Sound, was reused for the same purpose in the Second World War, and sections of it are now open to visitors.

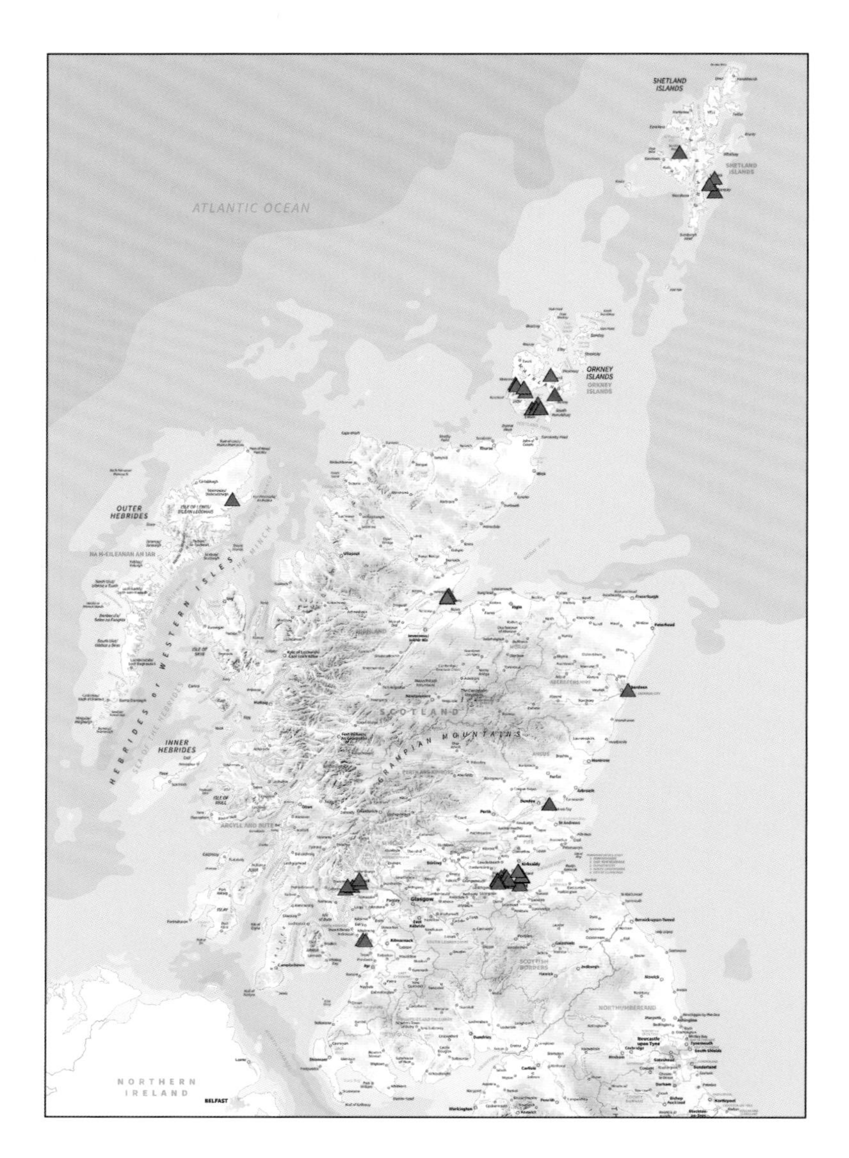

measures were needed. Scapa Flow in Orkney and the Cromarty Firth were chosen as the other Scottish bases for the Grand Fleet at the start of the conflict. Neither anchorage had any defence in place when this decision was made but batteries were at least under construction on the Sutors, the headlands at the entrance to the Cromarty Firth.

Artillery batteries were the primary form of defence along the Scottish coast. Coast defence formed an arm of the Royal Artillery, although at Scapa Flow and at Cromarty gun crews used Royal Naval and Royal Marine personnel. The batteries ranged from single guns to large complexes across entire islands like Inchkeith in the Forth estuary. Guns varied from 4 inch calibre quick firing (QF) guns for defence against fast vessels to 9.2 inch calibre guns with a range of more than sixteen miles that were intended to tackle enemy battleships. At Scapa Flow, relatively light 3 pounder and 12 pounder guns were brought ashore from ships to provide defence while the more permanent emplacements were constructed. By the time hostilities came to an end in 1918, there were around fifty-seven coast artillery batteries in place across Scotland, including up to twenty-three on the Forth and fifteen protecting Scapa Flow.

Coast defence required more than just artillery to be effective. Defence Electric Light (DEL) positions were established at batteries and at nearby strategic points: they had high-powered searchlights with fixed or movable beams, which could illuminate targets for the guns at night. Fire Control Posts allowed coordinated, targeted firing from numerous positions. Subterranean magazines protected the dangerous explosive shells and the charges that propelled them from enemy attack. Landward defences were also established – firing trenches, machine-gun emplacements, blockhouses, pillboxes and barbed wire entanglements – to prevent or delay coast artillery falling into enemy hands in the event of invasion. The entrances to many ports and naval anchorages were protected by controlled minefields. Large numbers of mines were attached to seabed anchors at varying depths to deal with ships of different sizes. These could be detonated singly or in groups from a control station on shore. Maps of the minefields on the Clyde and on the Tay still survive.

Although none of Scotland's coast defences ever saw any significant action, the often remote and exposed locations held their own difficulties and dangers. One man, stationed on the tiny island of Switha in Orkney, described one such incident:

Life was pretty grim on that lonely island outpost. There was no harbour or even a jetty. In stormy weather you were reduced to 'iron rations' because the provision boat couldn't get in. Oil fuel for the searchlights had to be floated ashore attached to ropes.

One dark night when it was snowing hard and blowing a blizzard, Tom Bowlin, a Royal naval Volunteer Reserve man, set off across the island to relieve the man on the searchlight there at the other

end. The man he was to relieve, Lomax, had been on the first watch, from 4pm to midnight.

Half an hour later came a phone call from Lomax to say Tom had not yet arrived. It was after midnight, so our small party set out, strung along a rope to which each man was secured so there would be no disappearing in drifts. In this way, each carrying a hurricane lantern we combed the length and breadth of the island, but without result.

Next morning he was found in a huddled heap on a rock at the bottom of the high and almost perpendicular cliff. Tom must have walked straight over the cliff edge in the snow, and only a few yards from his destination. When picked up he was dead from injuries and exposure.

When the war began Britain was ill-prepared for a deadly new technology that would change the face of naval warfare forever – the submarine. Although submarines had existed in some form for centuries, it was only in the nineteenth century that they became viable. By the advent of the First World War, sophisticated engineering was available and novel offensive strategies were being developed to take advantage of this form of warfare. Coast defence batteries could protect against fire from the deck gun of a submarine but there was little protection from torpedo attack. The effectiveness of submarine warfare quickly became clear and attention was focused on ways to counter the danger to ships at sea and in port. At sea, for example, aerial reconnaissance came into play and new weaponry was developed, such as delayed fuse timers on shells fired into the sea at submerged German submarines. In 1916 convoy systems were reintroduced to guard allied ships carrying vital supplies crossing the Atlantic. At the major anchorages, physical barriers to submarines such as boom defence nets were introduced. Before the war, the Admiralty had rejected the idea of boom defences. Its adoption in Britain can largely be credited to one man, Captain Donald John Munro. As Senior Naval Officer for the Cromarty base, Munro authorised the creation of a boom defence net despite the Admiralty's reservations. His design comprised a 'net' of steel cable, hanging below timber floats from the surface, and connected to trawlers or other small ships at each end, allowing it to be moved when required. The success of the system at Cromarty swiftly led to it being used by the Admiralty on a wider scale. 'Cromarty model booms' were subsequently installed at all the major anchorages in Scotland.

Additional elements were also developed to prevent enemy access from both submarines and surface vessels. At Scapa Flow, for example, obsolete ships known as blockships were deliberately sunk to act as barriers across various channels into the main anchorage. By far the most unique and substantial barrier against enemy vessels was built in Clestrain Sound, part of the western approach to Scapa Flow between the mainland of Orkney and the island of Graemsay. A substantial framework of steel rails was welded together to create a 'hurdle'. These 'hurdles' were then transported one by one and sunk in the channels, to form a nearly continuous barrier. The 'Clestrain Hurdles' as they were called were so effective that after the war a channel had to be cut through the blockage they made to allow peacetime shipping to pass through. The remains of these massive metal frames still survive on the seabed.

When America entered the war in 1917 the US Navy began to play a major role in the war at sea by providing Atlantic convoy escorts and supporting combat operations. In Scotland the United States also established two bases at Inverness and Invergordon to support their operations in the North Sea. Their main purpose was to lay the North Sea Mine Barrage, which was an ambitious plan to prevent or restrict German U-boats access to the Atlantic. The 'Barrage' was a minefield stretching across the North Sea for around 230 miles between Orkney and the west coast of Norway. It was an idea which had been considered earlier in the war but which was simply set aside as unaffordable until America joined the conflict. After the end of the war, several ships of the US Navy remained in Scotland to assist with the clearance of the 70,117 mines that had been laid.

Today the surviving elements of the coast batteries are generally the most prominent and visible reminder of the naval war in Scotland. At a few of the sites, such as St Kilda and Vementry on Shetland, the original guns remain in place. At sites like Kinghorn in Fife and the Sutors at Cromarty, the Defence Electric Light emplacements can still be found on the shoreline. The remains of additional buildings such as magazines are common survivals, as found at Hoxa Head, South Ronaldsay and Ness Battery, outside Stromness, both on Orkney. Fire Control posts also survive at a number of sites including at Cloch Point on the Clyde. Other prominent reminders of the naval war survive in Scotland, although less visible than most. On the seabed of Scapa Flow are seven remaining ships of the German High Seas Fleet scuttled there in June 1919. Also on the seabed are other vessels from the war such as the HMS *Vanguard* and the German submarine UB-116, destroyed when attempting to enter Scapa Flow secretly in 1918.

THE CLESTRAIN HURDLES ↓
Scapa Flow Landscape Partnership

The extremely strong currents through the western entrance to Scapa Flow prevented the use of standard boom defences, as the floating nets and their anchor vessels could not reliably hold a position. These giant metal frames, each more than nine metres wide and more than twenty metres high, were constructed on land, before being placed in a line across the mile wide width of Clestrain Sound, restricting access for both submarines and surface ships. After the war, an icebreaker ship was required to cut a channel through the blockage for peacetime shipping. The remains of these massive metal frames still survive on the seabed.

ANTI-SUBMARINE BOOMS
Imperial War Museum, London

One of the anti-submarine booms in operation at Scapa Flow. The small vessels used to tow and manoeuvre the net can be seen, with the timber floats stretching between them.

SOUTH SUTOR BATTERY, CROMARTY
RCAHMS

Excavation works for the construction of gun no.1 at the South Sutor battery, Cromarty. The brick foundations for the magazine are clearly visible.

HIDING IN PLAIN SIGHT

Imperial War Museum, London

Cecil King's painting, *Dazzled Ships at Leith,* depicts two merchant ships in the harbour painted with 'dazzle' camouflage. The brainchild of the artist, Norman Wilkinson, the camouflage consisted of vibrant geometric patterns, often brightly coloured. The aim was not to hide the ship, a feat that is next to impossible in the vast expanses of the ocean, but to disrupt the outline of the ship. It was believed that this made it more difficult for enemy vessels to estimate the type, size, speed and direction of vessels they were intending to attack.

GHOST SHIPS IN THE SAND
Richard Welsby, licensor SCRAN

The remains of a First World War blockship in Orkney. Blockships were used to obstruct access through shallower channels into the harbours. While many of the First World War blockships around Orkney survive even today, they failed in their purpose on the night of 14 October 1939. After navigating past the rusting hulks on the eastern entrance to Scapa Flow, the German U-boat U47 sank HMS *Royal Oak*, which had been in action at Jutland in 1916, along with 833 of her crew.

HMS VANGUARD ↓

Orkney Islands Council, licensor SCRAN

HMS *Vanguard*. The *Vanguard* had come through the Battle of Jutland unscathed, but late at night on 9 July 1917, while anchored in Scapa Flow, the ship was completely destroyed when the cordite in one of the magazines exploded by accident. The force of the blast threw one of the battleship's 12 inch gun turrets around a mile from the ship. One diver who helped with the salvage after the accident described bodies of sailors still in their hammocks within the remains of the ship. Another sailor described the search for survivors:

All hands were called on our ship and every boat was lowered to see if there were any survivors. I was in the cutter's crew and we were detailed to go ashore on Flotta Island. All the heather and gorse had been set alight by debris blown ashore from the Vanguard and we had to beat out the fire with single sticks. Whilst going ashore we were going through masses of thick oil. Clothing, sailors' ditty boxes, arms and legs, but no survivors.

The wreck is afforded statutory protection as a designated war grave under the Protection of Military Remains Act, 1986.

LORD KITCHENER ↗

Imperial War Museum, London

Lord Kitchener boarding HMS *Iron* Duke, Admiral John Jellicoe's flagship, in Scapa Flow on 5 June 1916. This is one of the last images of Kitchener, as HMS *Hampshire* sank later that day.

HOSPITAL SHIP →

Orkney Islands Council, licensor SCRAN

Stoker Frederick Cox and Royal Marine Private Williams, shown here on a hospital ship after the accident, were the only survivors of the 845 men aboard the HMS *Vanguard* when she exploded.

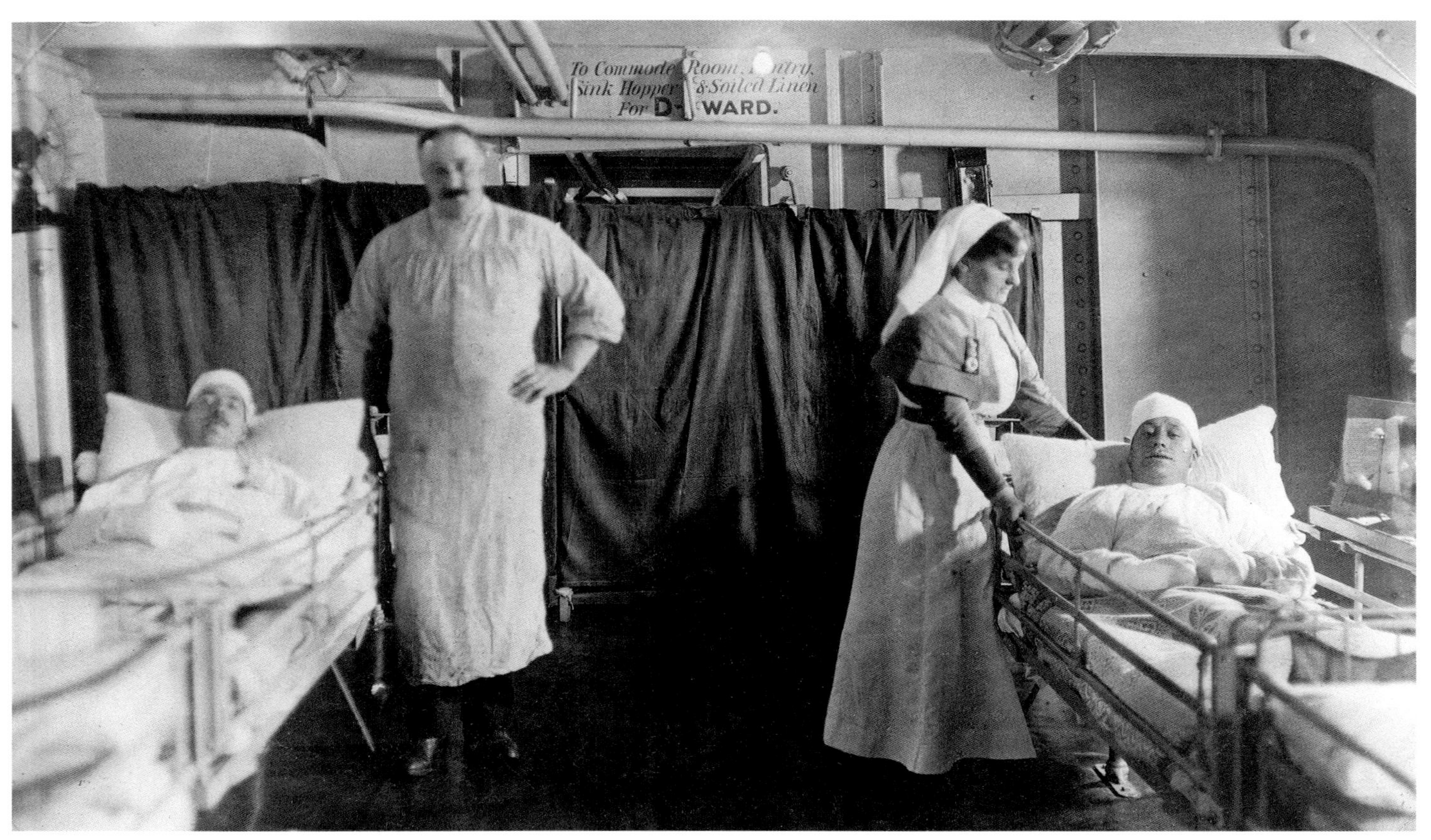
To Commode Room
Sink Hopper & Soiled Linen
For D WARD.

Fortress Forth

TRENCH WARFARE
Historic Scotland, Edinburgh

A First World War firing trench on the island of Inchkeith, with Edinburgh visible in the background. While the big guns of the artillery could defend against enemy ships, they were vulnerable to assault by enemy infantry assault. It was feared that enemy troops would land near the coast artillery batteries, to destroy or capture them, putting the guns out of action and allowing enemy ships to pass unhindered and attack the strategic assets beyond. To prevent this, the batteries were provided with their own defences. On Inchkeith these defences included blockhouses, machine guns and firing trenches such as this one, which is a part of the defences of the southern tip of the island.

The Firth of Forth was the most heavily defended anchorage in Scotland during the First World War. In the early twentieth century its strategic value increased with extensive plans to construct a new dockyard and naval base at Rosyth along with other bases at Granton and Port Edgar. At the outbreak of the war, development of the dockyards was incomplete but at least six batteries were in place. In order to protect these new strategic assets and others such as the Forth Bridge, a major construction effort took place to build defences further out in the estuary. Following the principle of defence in depth, three major lines of defence were established. An inner line ran immediately east of the Forth Bridge with batteries at Dalmeny, Hound Point and the island of Inchgarvie in the shadow of the bridge. A middle line stretched from Braefoot Point in Fife to Cramond Island and included the islands of Inchmickery and Inchcolm. The outer line ran between the batteries at Kinghorn and Pettycur in Fife to the island of Inchkeith and the port of Leith in Edinburgh. Later in the war, some of the guns from the inner line were transferred to the middle and outer lines to strengthen their defences.

Anti-submarine booms stretched between the islands and the shoreline in all three lines of defence, and the batteries were provided with Defence Electric Lights to illuminate targets at night. The batteries along the shoreline were also furnished with landward defences including blockhouses, pillboxes and barbed wire entanglements to protect them from assault by enemy ground forces. Although a vital part of the war effort and crucial to the defence of the bases upriver, serving on one of the islands in the Forth would have been a lonely existence. Whatever could be done to alleviate this would have been welcomed. The men stationed on Inchgarvie would often take a rowing boat to South Queensferry while off-duty in an attempt to relieve the sense of isolation they felt on the island. A soldier stationed on Inchkeith describing himself as 'an Inchkeith Limpet' wrote a poem, part of which describes the boredom and misery of his experience:

NAVAL BATTERIES
National Archives, Kew

This plan of the Firth of Forth shows the location of the coast artillery batteries on all three of the defence lines. Significant remains can still be seen at all of these positions, with the exception of the battery at Leith Docks on the bottom right of the plan.

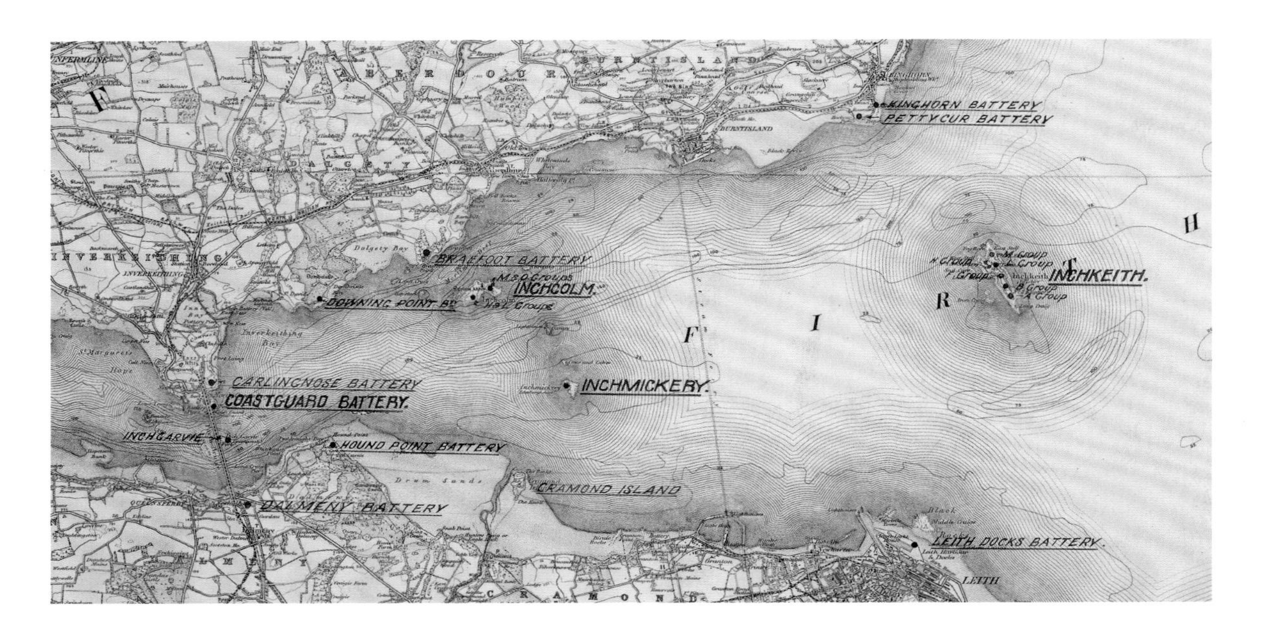

There are no clubs or music halls,
There are no shops or market stalls,
But when it rains, the water FALLS,
At Inchkeith.

A substantial number of the Forth defences remain in place today. On the inner line, the abandoned buildings of Inchgarvie can be seen from the trains passing over the bridge above, and significant remains can be seen at all of the other inner line batteries. The middle line contains extensive survival of all its batteries with clearly visible remains on Inchcolm. At Inchmickery the defences of this tiny island make it resemble a warship. Of the outer line, elements still exist of all sections except the battery at Leith. Remains on the island of Inchkeith, which was the headquarters of Forth defence strategy are particularly well preserved and significant, with the island utilised and built upon for defence on many occasions from the sixteenth century until well after the Second World War and with remains surviving from all these periods.

As the islands of the Forth and its estuary shoreline batteries are visible from almost anywhere in the Firth of Forth, the local people would have seen the vast effort being expended to defend the harbours upstream and would have witnessed the Royal Navy's movements on a daily basis. They may have seen the sinking of the HMS *Campania* on 5 November 1918. And, some of them will have watched later that month as the German High Seas Fleet was led into captivity. The escorting Royal Navy ships had every available gun loaded and aimed at their assigned German ship, in case of any attempt at treachery, although the German Fleet's guns had been completely disabled as requested. The occasion was described by John Paul Elliot, a sailor in the US Navy:

We were there when the ships came in, when the German ships surrendered. They all came in the Firth of Forth and dropped anchor. We didn't get too close to them, and they didn't get too close to us. I could see they were in a pretty run-down condition – they didn't look as though they'd been maintained. It was a kind of sad thing to see all these immense ships come in there and you know, just surrender like that. They looked so bedraggled to me, they just looked beaten, that's the way they impressed me. They didn't look like fighting ships any more.

PORT EDGAR

Scottish Life Archive, licensor SCRAN

Destroyers docked at Port Edgar. Despite the early belief that the Royal Navy would have a major role to play in the outcome of the war, in the end there was only a single large naval battle between the two opposing fleets, at Jutland on 31 May 1916. It resulted in more than 8,500 dead and twenty-three ships sunk between the two sides. Although the German fleet never again attempted to leave harbour, it was at best a pyrrhic victory for the British, whose losses were considerably higher. One man who witnessed the fleet returning to Scapa Flow after the battle described the scene as the battered fleet passed:

Our battery was placed right on the point of the island of Flotta. I was on duty when the Fleet came in from the Battle of Jutland. It was about 4 AM. It was a sad sight. No flags flying, no bands playing, but some battleships with their 12-inch guns cocked up in the air. Some of them with covers over the places where they had been hit. Especially the cruisers and destroyers, who I believe had many dead aboard.

THE NAVAL BASE AT GRANTON
Imperial War Museum, London

John Lavery's painting *Twilight, the Naval Base, Granton: Booms Guarding the Forth are Seen in the Distance* of the naval base at Granton. Granton was the base for the small ships that patrolled the anti-submarine booms and hunted enemy submarines on the east coast. It was also the base for the Q-ships – merchant ships with hidden guns used as decoys to lure U-boats to the surface (most ships were sunk not by torpedoes but by the submarine's gun). Many U-boats were sunk after thinking the Q-ships from Granton were an easy target.

INCHGARVIE
Imperial War Museum, London

The defences on Inchgarvie, seen from the Forth Bridge. As well as the batteries, the associated remains such as oil tanks, engine rooms and accommodation buildings are also visible. As the battery was not reused after the First World War, many of these structures survive unaltered on the island today.

HOUND POINT
National Archives, Kew

A plan of the defences at Hound Point near South Queensferry in 1916. Despite the highly functional nature of these structures, they were not without comforts, as can be seen in the detail of the blockhouse in the top centre of the image, which shows a stove provided for the resident garrison's use.

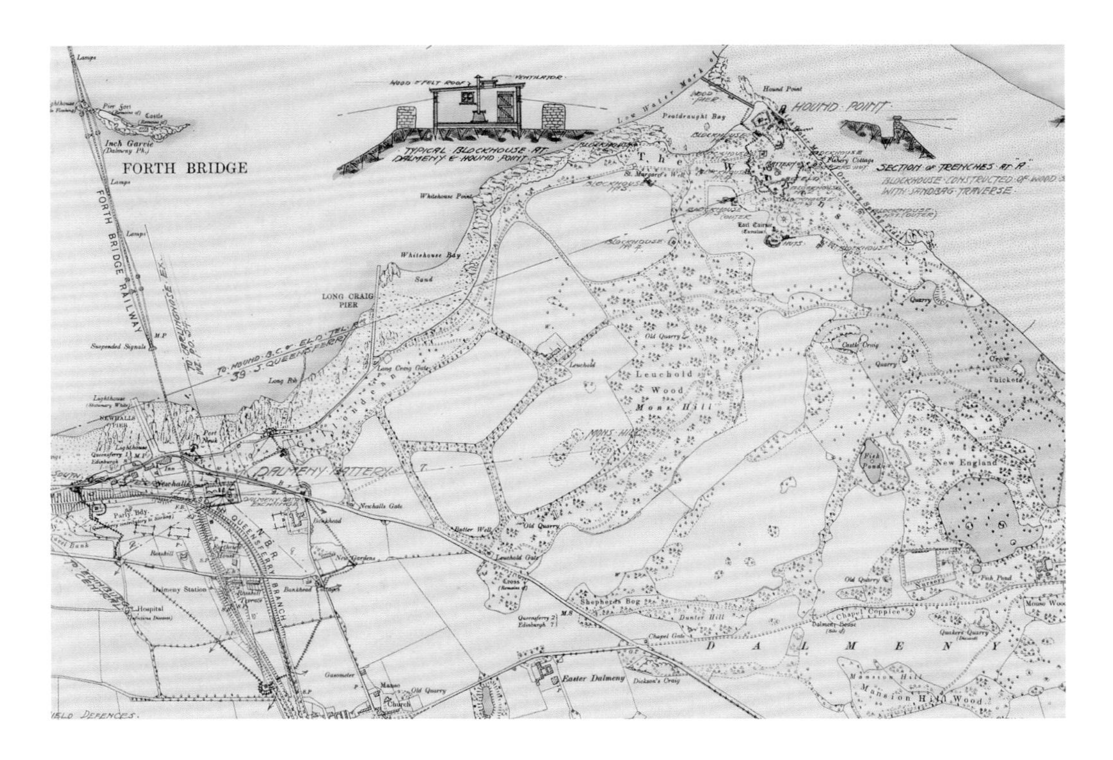

INCHKEITH ↓
National War Museum, National Museums of Scotland, Edinburgh

Nurses and soldiers pose for a photograph outside accommodation huts on Inchkeith.

INCHGARVIE →
Imperial War Museum, London

A gunner of the Royal Garrison Artillery on duty at Inchgarvie.

THE SINKING OF THE *CAMPANIA* →
Scotsman Publications Ltd, licensor SCRAN

The aircraft carrier HMS *Campania* sinking off Burntisland. The ship had been converted from a Cunard liner into one of the first aircraft carriers early in the war. On the morning of 5 November 1918, anchored off Burntisland in Fife, she began to drag her anchor in a gale. She collided with two other ships as she moved and breached her hull. Although her entire crew were rescued, HMS *Campania* sank that afternoon. The wreck is now designated as a Historic Marine Protected Area.

The War in the Air

AERIAL FATALITIES
Imperial War Museum, London

Squadron Commander Edwin Dunning, in his Sopwith Pup, making his fatal attempt at landing on HMS *Furious* on 7 August 1917. The HMS *Furious* began construction in 1915 as a light battle cruiser but, before completion, she was partially converted into one of the world's first aircraft carriers, with a flying off deck installed in the place of her forward guns. At the time, aircraft carriers were designed to allow planes to launch from the flying off deck, but not to land on the ship, instead flying to a terrestrial air station. While the *Furious* was deployed in Scapa Flow, tests were made on the possibility of landing on the ship. While the ship sailed at speed around the harbour, Commander Dunning made several attempts to land on the vessel and succeeded in doing so on 2 August. Unfortunately, a few days later an attempt to repeat this historic achievement cost him his life.

It was just eleven years before the First World War that the Wright Brothers flew the world's first aeroplane, yet this new invention would become a decisive weapon by the end of hostilities. Initially, reconnaissance flights provided military generals with a new perspective on the vast battle lines but by the end of the war aircraft could easily strike at targets far into enemy territory. Aerial combat grew in scale from chance encounters to enormous dogfights. Aircraft designs developed from plans of flimsy and frequently dangerous contraptions to far more sophisticated, lethal fighting machines. But in Scotland land-based fighter aircraft were the least significant element of the war in the air. Scotland was beyond the range of all German aeroplanes including the Gotha bombers that attacked southern England and there were few forays by Zeppelins. Aviation in Scotland in the first years of the war was exclusively in support of the war at sea.

Naval and terrestrial reconnaissance was significantly improved by the use of aerial observation. In Scotland, large airships flew from a range of sites, including East Fortune in the Lothians, Caldale in Orkney and Lenabo in Aberdeenshire, and the enormous sheds required to store them can be traced at several places, along with other parts of the airship stations. Ships were provided both with seaplanes and with kite balloons (unpowered observation balloons which could be towed high over the ships, attached by a steel cable), which could allow an observer a much greater field of vision. Bases and equipment had to be provided for the storage on land of kite balloons, and for the manufacture and storage of the hydrogen gas used to fill them, and these appeared in places as far apart as Lerwick in Shetland and the Rosyth naval base on the Forth. Kite balloons were also deployed from Caldale; one veteran of the station described an incident when the weather got the better of the kite balloon crews:
One gusty day a balloon broke free. The last unfortunate man to hold on to his guy rope was carried up 30 feet and fell, injuring his spine.
I was ordered to chase the balloon on my motorcycle to report where it went to. This I did with gusto

AIR STATIONS

Contains Ordnance Survey Data

This map shows all of the air stations in operation across Scotland. Stations for the use of airships, seaplanes and land based fixed-wing aircraft were to be found across the country. Some of the sites, shown in black on the map, were simply empty fields, to be used as emergency landing-strips whenever required, while those in blue were more substantive stations, with structures such as hangars, workshops and accommodation built on the site.

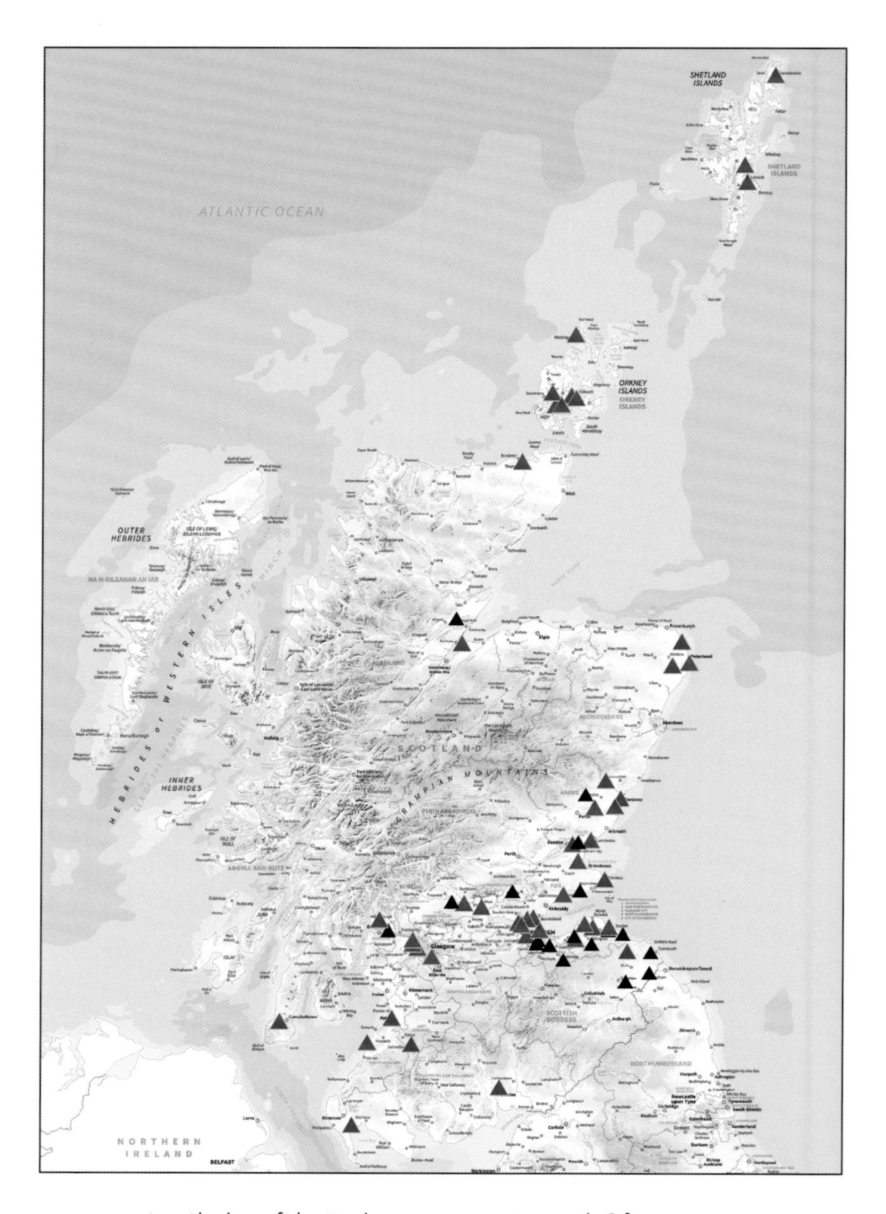

at full throttle and managed to keep it in sight to the north end of the Island, until my exhaust valve burnt out and I could only report that it was heading due north and making excellent progress.

The earliest airfields within Scotland were very different to the airports we recognise today. There was, for example, no need for built runways as grassy fields provided ample landing grounds. Nonetheless, evidence for aerial warfare does survive across the country. Fixed-wing aircraft flew from a total of forty-three sites across Scotland, with much of the activity related to training for pilots, observers and air-gunners. Montrose was the first military air station in Britain, and today some of its original buildings house the Montrose Air Station Heritage Centre. Opened in 1913, it was used particularly from 1916 onwards as a base for training pilots for the Royal Flying Corps and for the US Army Air Force; a task which it also undertook in the Second World War for the Royal Air Force. The graves of some RFC pilots who were lost during the war can be found in nearby Sleepy Hillock Cemetery.

Among the other forty-three fixed-wing aircraft sites used during the war were Crail and Leuchars in Fife, Turnhouse (now Edinburgh Airport) as well as locations in East Lothian from Drem to East Fortune, now the home of the National Museum of Flight. The luxury Turnberry Hotel near Ayr was commandeered for use both as officers' quarters for the air training station on the adjacent golf course and as a reception hospital for wounded personnel.

No 77 Home Defence Squadron was based in central Scotland and established many emergency landing-grounds in Edinburgh (including areas now under the buildings of the city), East Lothian and Fife. Even if action from German aircraft might be thought unlikely, nevertheless anti-aircraft guns were installed although the majority of these were essentially temporary. Sometimes near an air station it would be possible to see a heavy machine gun or a gun mounted on the back of a lorry. There were at least five sites in Scotland where more permanent anti-aircraft batteries were constructed. Of these, the best surviving example is on Orkney, at the eastern end of the small island of Burray. Others were located at Carness, also on Orkney, at Whiteforeland Point, Fort Matilda, Greenock, as well as at both the Rosyth and Crombie naval armaments depots in Fife.

One of the most substantial sites associated with early aerial warfare in Scotland survives at Loch Doon in Ayrshire, where a large aerial gunnery school was established from 1916. Much of the site was submerged in 1930 when the local reservoir was built, but evidence of its buildings remain around the edges of the loch and can also be seen from the air.

MONTROSE AIR STATION
Montrose Air Station Museum Trust, licensor SCRAN

Montrose Air Station in use during the First World War. The hangars visible in the background of this image still survive on the site today, along with a number of other structures from the station.

EXPERIMENTS AT LOCH DOON
Bruce/Leslie Collection, licensor SCRAN

One of the sites associated with aerial warfare was at Loch Doon and many experiments were carried out there. The photograph shows a BE2C biplane which has been fitted with an experimental float system for testing on the loch.

AIRSHIPS AT EAST FORTUNE
National Museum of Flight, National Museums of Scotland, licensor SCRAN

The airship R34 at East Fortune, with another smaller airship, NS7 overhead. In the background are the giant sheds built to house the airships on the ground. Shortly after the war, the R34 completed the first direct flight across the Atlantic Ocean to New York, having departed from East Fortune.

EDINBURGH BOMBED
Imperial War Museum, London

Late on 2 April 1916, two Zeppelins, L14 and L20, arrived in the skies over the Forth. Their main target was the Rosyth naval base, but unable to reach it due to the defences, they instead turned towards Edinburgh and Leith, where they began dropping high explosive and incendiary bombs. Among the areas hit were a bonded warehouse in Leith, which was destroyed by the resulting blaze, Castle Rock, the Grassmarket and a hotel on Lothian Road, along with numerous private houses and tenement buildings. In the end, a machine gun on Arthur's Seat opened fire on the airships, forcing them to withdraw. (The gunfire does not appear to have damaged either Zeppelin, which was a blessing in disguise, as if either ship had crashed or caught fire, it would probably have done more damage than the bombs they had dropped.) In the end, many buildings were damaged, and at least nine people killed, with more than twenty injured.

BOMB DAMAGE OUTSIDE THE WHITE HART HOTEL IN THE GRASSMARKET AREA OF EDINBURGH.
Imperial War Museum, London

BOMB DAMAGE TO MCCALLUM'S STORE ON NICOLSON STREET, EDINBURGH.
Imperial War Museum, London

HMS KING GEORGE V ↓

Imperial War Museum, London

HMS *King George V* was one of four King George V class battleships built for the Royal Navy shortly before the outbreak of war. She is seen here underway at Scapa Flow in 1917, towing an observation balloon overhead. A boom defence net can be seen in the background.

CALDALE AIRSHIP STATION →

National Museum of Flight, National Museums of Scotland, licensor SCRAN

Caldale was, during the First World War, one of four stations established for military airships to patrol the sea lanes off Scotland, to search for enemy submarines and to escort convoys. It was established in July 1916 in a hollow west of Kirkwall, sheltered to some extent from all but easterly winds. The first airship shed, for anti-submarine scouting airships and measuring 45 metres by 13 metres seems to have been built in 1916. A second much larger shed for coastal patrol type airships was completed by September 1917. The areas in front of the massive doors of the sheds were protected by six high 'wind-screens' to prevent the balloons being blown about when they were pulled from their sheds. The photograph shows Caldale Airship Station shortly after the war. The massive sheds that housed the airships lie beyond the accommodation, offices and workshops of the base.

LUXURY RESORT AIDS THE WAR EFFORT →

The Turnberry Resort

The luxury Turnberry Hotel was commandeered for use as officers' quarters for the air training station and as a reception hospital. The golf links at Turnberry were also transformed into one of Scotland's largest air stations, with four large aircraft hangars, workshops, canvas hangars and training huts.

Defending the Home Front

NORTH BERWICK PILLBOX

Historic Scotland, Edinburgh

This pillbox, overlooking the shore at West Links just outside North Berwick, is one of many found across Scotland, dating to both the First and Second World Wars. This example is a highly unusual one, with a number of interesting features, not least of which is the inscription of a date in the concrete of 1919. There is no clear reason why a pillbox would have been built here after the Armistice, yet a number of other architectural features of the structure are characteristically First World War in style, which suggests that the pillbox was indeed built after the fighting was ended and when most other defences were being removed.

An enormous network of Second World War anti-invasion sites survive in Scotland and are a testament to the fear of attack on the Home Front that gripped the country in 1940. Far less obvious and certainly less well known are remnants of a similar effort dating from the First World War. Fear that a German invasion might come from across the North Sea led to the construction of home defences on a considerable scale. These took the form of extensive barbed wire entanglements behind which firing trenches and pillboxes were built for infantrymen. The extent of these inland defences and the preparations involved in their construction has only recently come to light in the army records of Scottish Command held in the National Archives at Kew. The records mainly comprise large-scale maps showing the location of defensive features built in 1914-1916, although what is on the maps does not always match what was actually built. It is, nonetheless, proof that it was considered essential that there were plans to defend significant strategic assets. Major military sites such as the batteries at Fort Matilda and Portkil on the Clyde and naval bases as at Invergordon were provided with landward defences to prevent an enemy from seizing vital facilities. Physical remnants of these defences have recently been discovered around the North Sutor battery defending the entrance to the Cromarty Firth and pillboxes have been identified at Portkil Battery on the Clyde and at Kinghorn on the Forth. Similar systems were required for the protection of national industrial assets. For example, the Nobel Company's explosive works at Ardeer in North Ayrshire had its own coast artillery batteries, mainly to tackle enemy submarines that might attack from the estuary, as well as a defensive perimeter equipped with machine guns. The most extensive defences, however, were built not to protect individual assets such as batteries and factories, but to protect the city of Edinburgh. The East Lothian coastline with its sandy beaches, rolling agricultural landscape and major communication lines would have made this the ideal landing place for a German invasion. If Edinburgh were

BEACHES AT DUNBAR →

RCAHMS

Anti-invasion defences at Hedderwick links, just to the west of Dunbar. The same beach was defended again in 1940–2, and some of the visible features were reused in that period. The main element of the First World War defences is the winding trench visible running from [1–2], with another section at [3]. In addition, the land at [4] was used as a landing strip for aircraft practicing launching torpedoes in Belhaven Bay.

EAST LOTHIAN DEFENCES ↓

National Archives, Kew

A plan of the defences at Hedderwick links showing the network of trenches, redoubts and machine gun position. Section [1–2] and section [3] marked in the same place as the photograph.

captured then the major naval base at Rosyth would be under threat. Defences were built along the beaches most susceptible to invasion, particularly around Dunbar. Blockhouses were constructed just outside Edinburgh, at Musselburgh and West Pans. A ribbon of trenches, strong points and barbed wire fences stretched across the entire eastern edge of Edinburgh from the coast at Seafield all the way to Meadowfield Farm near Liberton and included the medieval Liberton tower as a strong point. These anti-invasion defences continued to be developed throughout the war and even beyond as shown by a pillbox at North Berwick, which is inscribed with the date 1919 in the concrete. Ultimately the effort expended in defence against invasion was, in practical terms, as unnecessary as similar attempts in the Second World War. Yet at the time, as the trenches were being dug and the barbed wire entanglements laid across the country, those who witnessed the preparations must have feared that the distant battles, until then known only in daily papers and British Pathé newsreels might one day be much closer at hand.

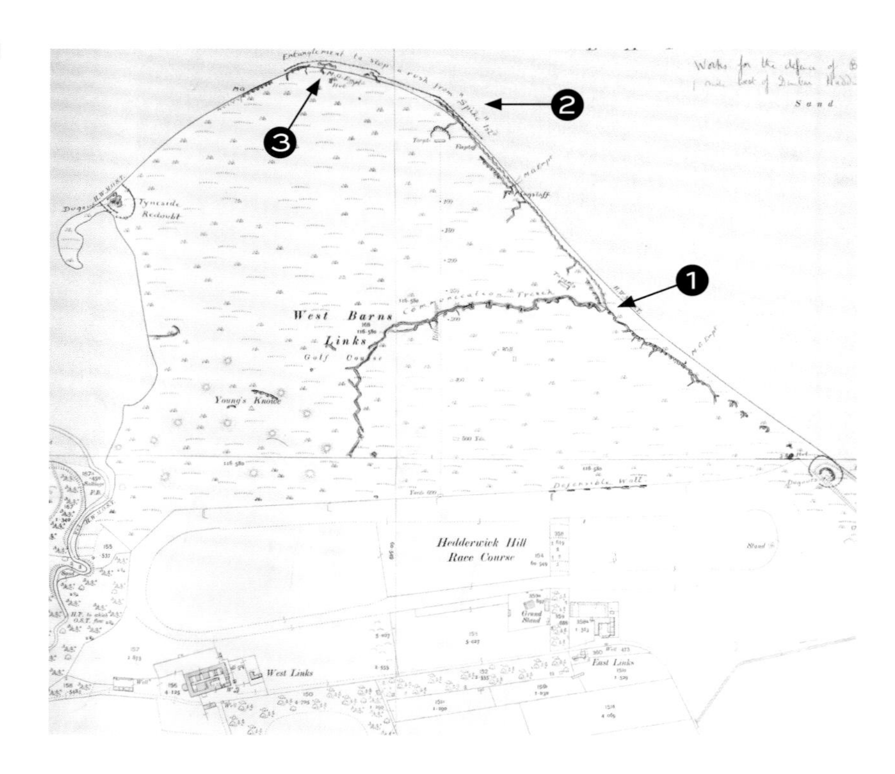

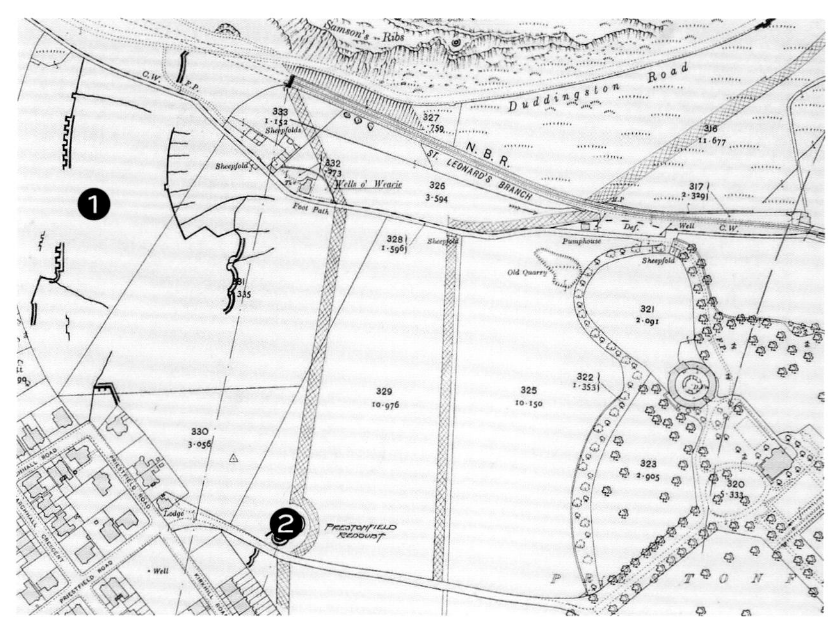

EDINBURGH DEFENDED →

National Archives, Kew

The plan shows the anti-invasion defences to the south of Arthur's Seat in Holyrood Park and Prestonfield Golf Course, Edinburgh. The blue-hatched areas represent barbed wire, while trenches which can be seen at [1] are still visible as earthworks. At [2] is the Prestonfield Redoubt, intended to be a strongpoint on the line. Two machine gun positions on Samson's Ribs may have fired on the Zeppelin that bombed Edinburgh in 1916.

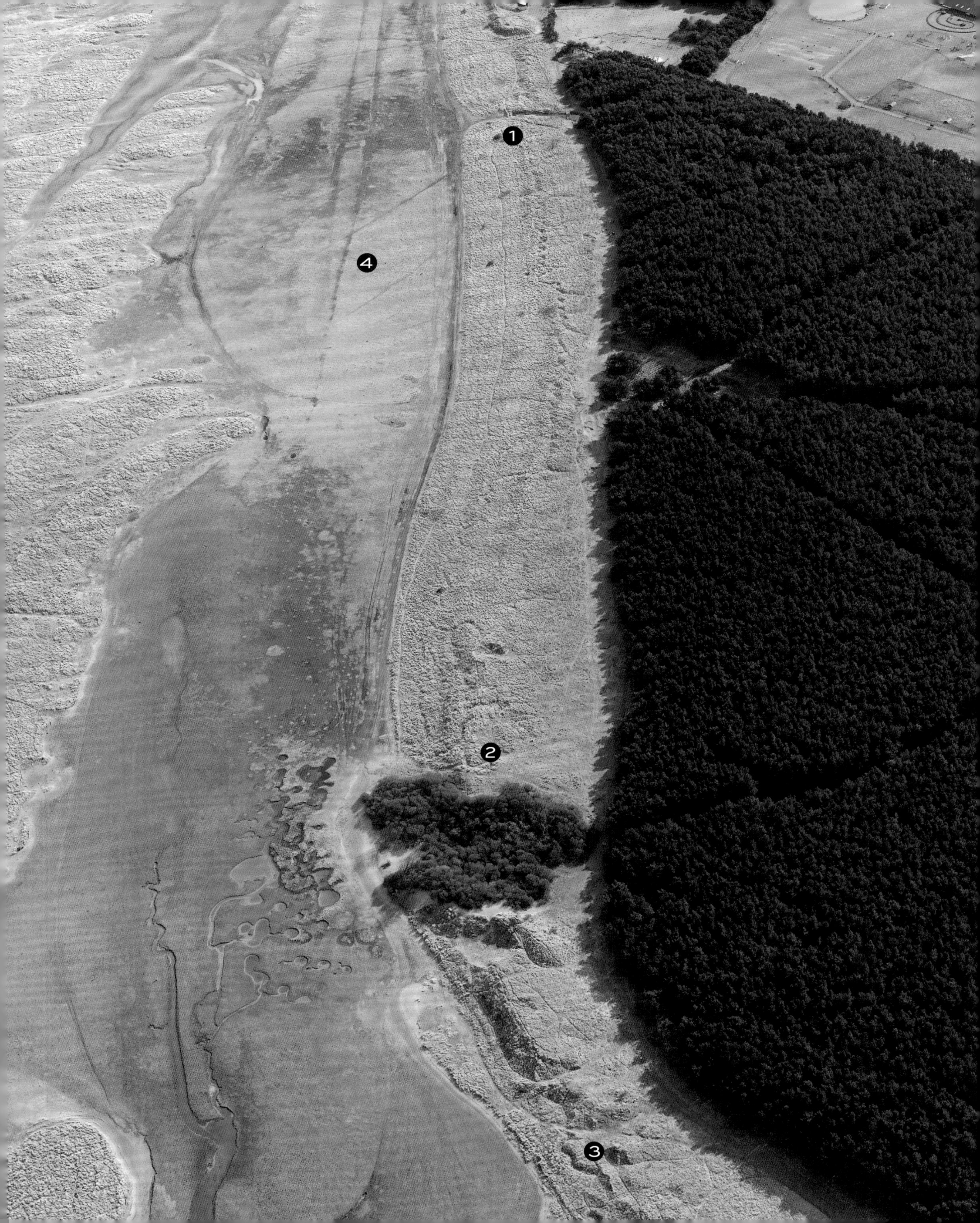
1
4
2
3

KINGHORN BATTERY
Historic Scotland, Edinburgh

The boundary wall of the coast artillery battery at Kinghorn in Fife. The line of rectangular holes in the wall are firing loopholes. These loopholes were intentionally built into the wall, so that the men of the battery could effectively defend it against an enemy attack from inland, while not exposing themselves to enemy gunfire at the same time. This battery was reused in the Second World War, and since that time the loopholes on the left half of the wall have been filled in, but the outline of each remains clear.

Preparing for Battle

TRAINING IN SHETLAND
Shetland Museum and Archives

Men in training at Fort Charlotte in Lerwick, Shetland. The strategic location of Shetland led to it being substantially fortified and it became home to large numbers of army and naval personnel throughout the First World War. It was vital to the war effort that the vast numbers of new and existing personnel were physically and mentally prepared, and these sailors are undergoing fitness training inside the fort. Fort Charlotte itself was first built in the 1600s to defend Lerwick harbour from attacks by the Dutch, before being rebuilt in its current form in 1781, during the height of the American War of Independence. It served in a variety of roles before going out of use. Today it is in the care of Historic Scotland and is open to the public.

At the start of the First World War, the British Army was far smaller than would be required for the coming conflict. The regular army excluding reservists had a total strength of only 247,432 men of which an estimated 20,000 came from Scotland. When war broke out many soldiers were on active service in the Empire. Scottish soldiers involved in the First World War can generally be classed in three ways: regular troops, who were the full time soldiers at the opening of the war, the territorial units, volunteer soldiers similar to the modern Territorial Army and also active at the outbreak of war, and the New Army units, created by Lord Kitchener specifically for the First World War and comprising civilian volunteers and later conscripted men.

Each regiment had its own depot located in or near its traditional recruiting ground. The depots provided barracks, equipment stores, training areas and housed relics such as the regimental colours. The ten Scottish regiments were split across nine depots in Scotland, with the King's Own Scottish Borderers depot just across the border in Berwick upon Tweed. Of these the most complete surviving Victorian depot is that of the Queen's Own Cameron Highlanders in Inverness. Glencorse near Edinburgh, Fort George in Inverness and Stirling Castle also survive in a substantive way (along with Berwick-upon-Tweed). All four of the Scottish examples are protected; Fort George and Stirling Castle are scheduled monuments in the care of Historic Scotland while the Queen's Own Cameron Highlanders' Barracks and Glencorse are listed buildings.

In addition to the regimental depots there were drill halls across Scotland serving local communities. Drill halls first appeared in Britain in the 1860s. They were originally constructed for training rifle or artillery volunteers and were generally paid for either by public subscription or local benefaction. The 1908 reforms that replaced the volunteers with the Territorial Army led to major building campaigns and by the time of the First World War many drill halls had expanded to include accommodation for

Regiment	Regimental Depot Location
King's Own Scottish Borderers	Berwick-upon-Tweed Barracks
Queen's Own Cameron Highlanders	Cameron Barracks, Inverness
Seaforth Highlanders	Fort George, Ardersier
Royal Scots	Glencorse Barracks, Penicuik
Argyll and Sutherland Highlanders	Stirling Castle
Highland Light Infantry	Maryhill Barracks, Glasgow
Gordon Highlanders	Castlehill Barracks, Aberdeen
Royal Scots Fusiliers	Ayr Barracks
Black Watch	Queen's Barracks, Perth
Cameronians (Scottish Rifles)	Hamilton Barracks

HOME DEPOTS
Historic Scotland, Edinburgh

The table to the left shows the home depots of the ten Scottish regiments of the British Army during the First World War. The depots at Glencorse and Fort George remain active garrisons for some of the battalions of the Royal Regiment of Scotland today.

DRILL HALLS
RCAHMS *and* Historic Scotland, Edinburgh

Two of the more elaborate drill halls found within Scotland. The timber drill hall at Golspie in Sutherland (top) and the Jardine Street drill hall in Glasgow (bottom). During the First World War, the drill halls became the most direct connection of many local communities to the events of the war. Today, many of these halls still play a part in the life of their local community as village halls and community centres.

resident instructors, administrative support and other facilities. Often buildings served more than one unit so that one drill hall might be the base for a company of territorial infantry and also for a territorial cavalry squadron, for example. There were at least 300 drill halls in use in Scotland during the First World War and more may have existed for which records have been lost or are currently unlocated. They vary widely in their architectural style from simple wooden huts and stone-built halls to extremely complex and elaborate buildings. Many of these buildings continue to survive. At Golspie the drill hall is a large timber building constructed in 1892. By 1914 it served as the headquarters of 5th Battalion Seaforth Highlanders as well as the drill station for A company of the battalion. The Jardine Street drill hall in Glasgow constructed in 1894 is an elaborate Tudor style building and in 1914 housed the 1st Field Company, Highland Divisional Royal Engineers and the Scottish Command of the Royal Engineer Signal Companies. The drill hall on Custom House Street in Ullapool is a much simpler rubble-built hall with a corrugated iron roof and an attached dwelling for the instructor; this was used both by the Lovat Scouts and the Seaforth Highlanders.

As well as depots and drill halls, barracks were required to accommodate the increasing numbers of soldiers. During the war some army barracks were purpose-built, such as those at Invergordon in Easter Ross and at Gourock on the Firth of Clyde. Other barracks were housed in existing buildings, which were requisitioned for the purpose, such as Dudhope Castle in Dundee. Most accommodation for serving personnel was required by the army but other sectors such as the navy also required facilities. There were naval barracks at Port Edgar on the Forth, opposite the Rosyth naval base. Additionally, accommodation camps were constructed at or near the various air stations created during the war and the remains of some of these can be seen at Loch Doon, Dalmuir and East Fortune in particular. A former infantry barracks in the centre of Montrose was used for part of the war to accommodate personnel from the air station at the north side of the town.

On top of housing the vast numbers of men, various branches of the military also had to prepare them for combat. Some aspects of a soldier's training, such as drill training, were conducted at the depots and drill halls of the regiments, but other activities required specific facilities. Training in marksmanship was usually conducted on purpose-built sites although many drill halls had indoor firing ranges. Outdoor ranges were built facing towards the sea, thick woodland or higher ground to ensure that any stray rounds missing the targets would be rendered harmless. Some firing ranges had been

PORT EDGAR
RCAHMS

One of the naval barracks buildings and the hospital at Port Edgar on the Forth. A range of buildings used in the First World War survive in this Category B listed complex, including barracks, wards and recreation buildings.

established long before the First World War for the use of the volunteer rifle units, others remained in operation many years after the war and a number of ranges are still in use today. Fort George has a range that has been in use since at least 1870 when it appeared on first editions of the Ordnance Survey maps. Elsewhere there are still visible traces of firing ranges at Dingwall in Inverness, at Cromarty at the mouth of the Cromarty Firth, at Melrose in the Scottish Borders and at Holyrood Park in Edinburgh.

The nature of conflict during the First World War also demanded a new and specific form of training for the infantry, namely, learning the tactics and dangers of trench warfare. Early in the war, soldiers would practise digging and strengthening the trenches and examples of these can be found across Scotland. As the war progressed and the frontlines became more static there was less need to construct new trenches. The training regimes changed to make use of the existing trenches to teach recruits the skills they would need in combat. Today, it is possible to see the remains of these training trenches at Dreghorn on the outskirts of Edinburgh as well as at Broomhill in Glasgow and Rhicullen near Invergordon. Others appear as archaeological features visible on aerial photographs as at Kinghorn in Fife. There are also trenches to be found in the vicinity of Stobs Camp, the largest training camp in Scotland, where New Army recruits trained alongside troops from Canada and other parts of the empire. Other sectors of

BARRACKS
RCAHMS

To accommodate the numbers of soldiers, many new army barracks were built such as those at Invergordon and Easter Ross. In addition, existing buildings such as Dudhope Castle in Dundee were requisitioned for use by the army.

the army also trained in Scotland, with artillery training at Barry Links near Carnoustie in Angus, for example. Nearby at Broughty Castle in Dundee from 1910 until after the war there was a coast artillery training school for the Royal Garrison Artillery. This was also the site of the major coast defence guns that protected the Tay. A non-firing practice battery first established in the nineteenth century was also maintained at Stornoway in the Outer Hebrides.

The aerial war required its own techniques for training recruits. Until the beginning of 1916 Montrose was the only Royal Flying Corps aerodrome in Scotland, the others were affiliated to the Royal Naval Air Service. During 1916 two Royal Flying Corps schools were established at Raploch in Stirling and at Turnhouse (now Edinburgh airport) and construction began on the aerial gunnery school at Loch Doon, where German prisoners of war were deployed to help with the construction. Loch Doon was disastrous in every sense, with an appalling choice of site and obsolete equipment. Costs spiralled for a project that in the end never trained a single gunner. From 1917 training for those involved in aerial warfare was much better organised and new air stations were established in Scotland at Gullane in East Lothian as well as at Crail and Leuchars in Fife. More advanced stations were opened at Turnberry, near Ayr where a gunnery school started up in 1917. Despite the rapid increase

FIRING RANGES AT FORT GEORGE
RCAHMS

The firing ranges at Fort George, which are still used for training. The lighter coloured strip of land running from [1] to [2] is one of the First World War ranges. The range to the left parallel to this may also have been in use at the time.

in importance of this new form of warfare, and the need for new pilots, the training failed to keep pace, and at some points in the war the life expectancy of a new pilot was as little as a few weeks.

While serving personnel in Scotland from all parts of the military spent most of their time between training and active service, it was recognised that they also needed time for social, sporting and leisure activities. Rest and keeping morale high was necessary, especially for the naval forces based on ships in Scottish harbours. At both Gretna near Dumfries and Invergordon in Easter Ross the local bars were placed under national control. This allowed monitoring and control of alcohol consumption by troops and civilian workers. At Rosyth in Fife the regular crews of the Battle Cruiser Fleet based there were able to play football onshore or enjoy a drink with comrades at a local 'wet' canteen established by McEwan's brewery. Officers of the Rosyth fleet meanwhile were frequently found in Edinburgh at a range of private members clubs, hotels and cinemas. At Scapa Flow much of the island of Flotta was given over to the Royal Navy to use for leisure pursuits. An 18-hole golf course was developed, along with football pitches, tennis courts and shooting ranges. The island also hosted the annual fleet boxing tournament each year. Much of the evidence of this aspect of Scapa Flow's wartime role has been lost, but on the summit of Roan Head stands one visible reminder: the ruinous remains of the YMCA built during the war for the use of naval personnel in the harbour. Many thousands of sailors came here to socialise and relax. Some of them would have spent their final hours ashore in this place of comfort before returning to their vessels and setting off on perilous voyages.

FIRING RANGES AT PATTERTON
West of Scotland Archaeology Service, licensor SCRAN

Rifle ranges were constructed across Scotland before the commencement of the First World War and were used for training purposes. Most no longer exist but trenches on the rifle range at Patterton, just outside Glasgow are still clearly defined.

TRENCHES
GUARD Archaeology Ltd

These First World War trenches survive in Dreghorn Woods, adjacent to Dreghorn Barracks in Edinburgh. Like other examples of this type of site, in the early part of the war, men would be trained in how to dig and support trenches such as these, but later they were solely used to teach men the techniques and tactics being used in trench warfare on the Western Front and elsewhere.
[top] One of the best surviving sections: the main dug-out or shelter, a square three metres by three metres with trenches on three sides.
[middle] A smaller dug-out.
[bottom] Part of the winding system of trenches. In some places the corrugated iron sheets supporting the trench sides still survive.

BROUGHTY CASTLE

RCAHMS

The coast battery and coast artillery and gunnery school at Broughty Castle near Dundee. Although this image was taken in 1932, most of the First World War site remains in place. The former 4.7 inch gun emplacements are located on the top of the earlier artillery fortification at [1], while the later 6 inch emplacements, with the guns still in place, are visible further east at [3]. The submarine mining station protecting the Tay and which later accommodated the gunnery school was housed in the buildings at [2].

BROUGHTY CASTLE
RCAHMS

A modern view of Broughty Castle. The concrete emplacements for the 4.7 inch guns can still be seen next to the castle itself, and the building adjacent to the road is the last surviving section of the former submarine mining station.

12 13 14 15
14 13 12

CONCERT PARTIES ↖
National War Museum, National Museums of Scotland, Edinburgh

Members of a concert party on the battle-cruiser HMS *Courageous*. Among the leisure activities available to personnel were concert parties such as this one, consisting of serving personnel who would put on entertainment for their comrades. They varied in quality, with larger ships and infantry formations having a wider talent pool to choose from, and in many cases holding auditions for the role. A highlight was always the performances of songs with rousing choruses which the audience could join in and forget their troubles for a short while.

ALL WORK AND NO PLAY ←
National War Museum, National Museums of Scotland

Men from the Royal Garrison Artillery taking their roles less seriously than their commanders would have likely preferred.

DOWN TIME AT SOUTH QUEENSFERRY ↑
Imperial War Museum, London

Sport played an important part during the war and football matches and rugby matches and golf tournaments were held in many different locations. Much of the island of Flotta at Scapa Flow was given over to the Royal Navy for leisure pursuits and the annual fleet boxing tournament was held there. Illustrated is a rugby match between a combined team from HMS *Australia* with HMS *New Zealand* and HMS *Repulse*. The Forth Bridge can be seen in the background.

BRISTOL SCOUTS
Dugald Cameron, licensor SCRAN

Dugald Cameron's painting *Bristol Scout D military biplane of No 43 Squadron at Raploch airfield Stirling 1916*, which the artist painted from a photograph. This field at Falloninch Farm was used as a training airfield later in the war, with the farm itself used as an officers' mess for the site. Stirling Castle and the Wallace Monument can be seen in the background.

THE YMCA AT FLOTTA

RCAHMS

The remains of the YMCA building on Flotta. The Young Men's Christian Association established thousands of recreation centres for troops across Europe. From those in quiet out-of-the-way areas to others just a few metres from the front lines, they were places where passing soldiers could find refreshment and some brief relaxation.

Dalmeny Street Drill Hall

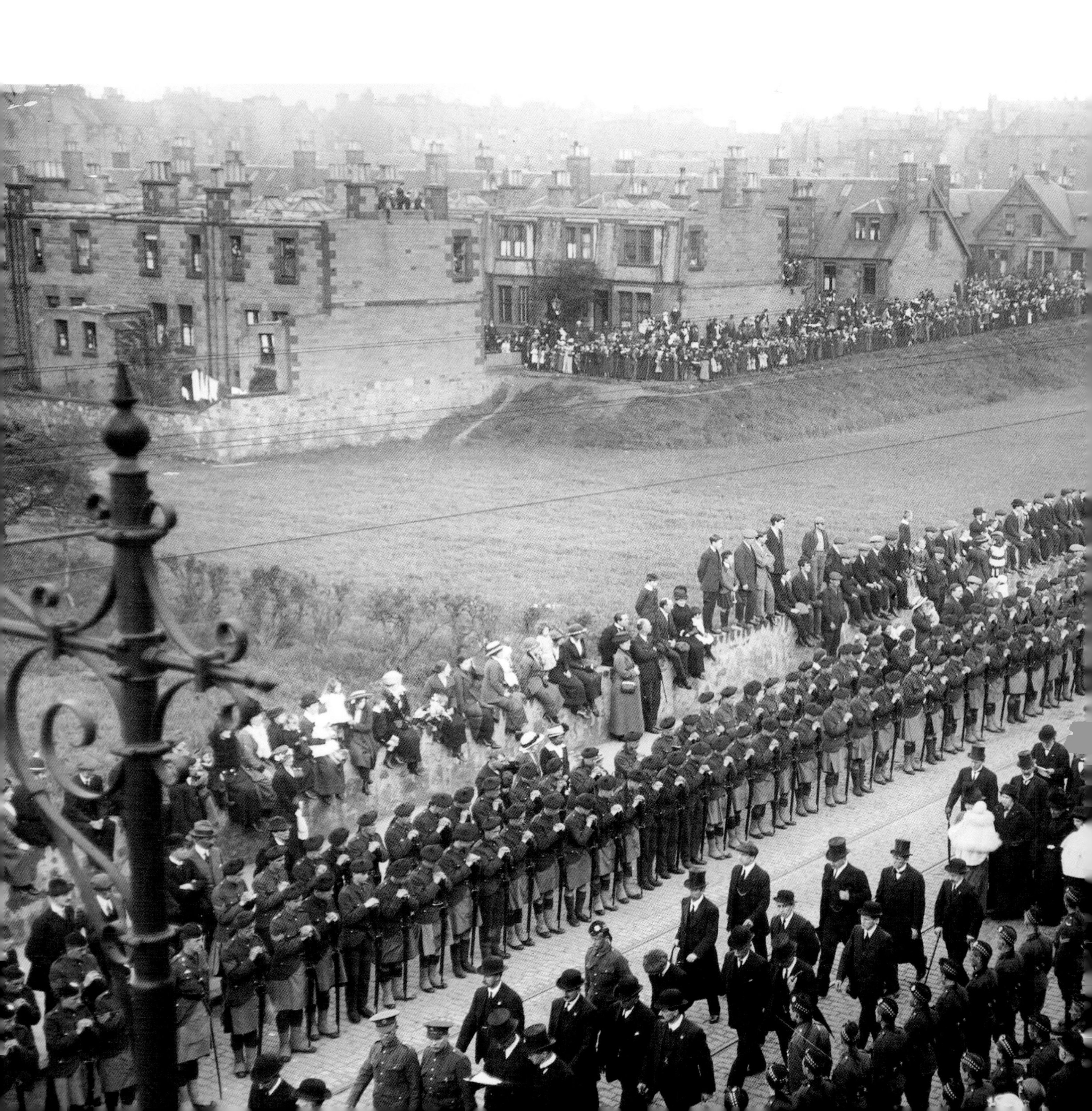

FUNERAL PROCESSION
Getty Images, licensor SCRAN

The funeral procession in Leith following the Quintinshill train crash. Many thousands of mourners turned out to pay their respects to the men of the 1/7th Battalion of the Royal Scots who had been killed less than a hundred miles from home, in one of the most tragic accidents of the war. The mass funeral of 100 of the dead took several hours to travel the short distance to the cemetery, and so many of the residents of the area attended that Leith was, in essence, holding an unofficial day of mourning for the young men of their community. The 214 men killed in the accident accounted for forty-two per cent of the battalion's casualties in the entire war, and they are listed now on a Roll of Honour on the memorial in Rosebank Cemetery.

One building in Dalmeny Street in Leith, to the north of Edinburgh, is an example of the central role drill halls played in the local community. Opened in 1901 the Dalmeny Street Drill Hall was designed in an Edwardian Baroque style by the architect Sir Robert Rowand Anderson. At the beginning of the First World War it was used by most of the companies of the 1/7th Battalion of the Royal Scots. This was one of seven territorial battalions attached to the regiment in 1914 and the battalion's title is inscribed above the central archway. Known as 'Leith's Own' the battalion was made up of local volunteers.

In the opening months of the war the battalion was in familiar territory while it served on the coast defences around Edinburgh as part of the Lothian Brigade. However in April 1915 the battalion was assigned to the 52nd Lowland Division, preparing to go to front lines at Gallipoli. Early in the morning of Saturday 22 May the men boarded two troop trains at Larbert bound for Liverpool and the ships ready to leave for the front lines. Due to a shortage of carriages, A and D company of Leith's Own occupied a train made of outdated gas-lit wooden carriages.

The men were in good spirits as they set off but many of them would never leave Scotland. Due to a mistake by signalmen shortly before 7am the train collided at high speed with a stationary local train at Quintinshill near Gretna. Seconds later a northbound express thundered into the wreckage, ploughing through the remains of the troop train and hitting many of the soldiers both inside and out of the carriages. Two stationary goods trains on adjacent tracks were also caught up in the carnage. The combination of the four damaged steam locomotives, shattered wooden carriages and the ruptured gas tanks of the troop train caused the wreckage to burst into a firestorm so hot it buckled the steel carriages of the express and caused the gas tanks to explode. A reporter on the scene described the horrifying sight before him:

In a moment all was terrible confusion. Engines were heaped upon one another, carriages telescoped and overturned, and others mounted one upon the other.

Men were hurled from the train – a fortunate few well clear – others clambered out from the wreckage as best they could. Many were pinned below the overturned carriages. Already the troop train and the leading carriages of the London train were ablaze. The men still on board were in a terrible plight. The successive collisions had effectively jammed the carriage doors. Exit that way was impossible. Windows refused to come down, and the glass had to be smashed before the men could get clear. Many men confessed that they did not know by what means or in what manner they got out.

Many people living nearby, having heard the crash, came rushing to help the survivors. An ambulance train was dispatched from Carlisle and other medical staff drove to the scene from Edinburgh and Carlisle. Emergency amputations were performed to free trapped victims although many would not survive the shock. The Carlisle fire brigade arrived two hours later around 9am, having been wrongly informed that the fire was extinguished an hour before. By the time they appeared nothing could be done. The fire burned for twenty-three hours.

At 4pm Colonel Peebles took a roll call of his men. Only sixty-five of almost 500 Royal Scots who had been on the train were present. The fire had destroyed the battalion muster roll and many bodies were too badly burned to identify. Others were completely consumed by the blaze. Accurate casualty figures are thus difficult to determine but it is estimated that around 215 of the battalion were killed and around 190 injured. This incident accounted for forty-two per cent of the battalion's casualties for the entire war. The survivors were eventually boarded onto another train further down the line and continued on to Liverpool, but on arrival they were almost all declared unfit for service following their trauma. Only Colonel Peebles and six other officers departed for Gallipoli with the half of the battalion who had been on the other train. Soon only 174 of the 1028 men of the 7th Battalion of the Royal Scots who had departed from Larbert were left. The rest had been wounded or killed. Back home in Leith as news of the disaster began to arrive, friends and relatives of the men in the battalion gathered outside the drill hall on Dalmeny Street, desperate for news of their loved ones. Eventually from an upstairs window the casualty list was read out, bringing more sorrow than relief to the

DALMENY STREET DRILL HALL
Historic Scotland, Edinburgh

The former drill hall at Dalmeny Street, Leith. Today it houses the Out of the Blue Arts and Education Trust, and remains a community hub for the residents of Leith.

SKELETON COACH
Scotsman Publications Ltd, licensor SCRAN

The aftermath of the accident. The carriage on the left has been completely destroyed by the fire.

↙ **RAILWAY CRASH**
Getty Images, licensor SCRAN

Some of the casualties being treated at the scene of the accident.

crowd below. The list was then displayed outside the hall. The day after the disaster the bodies of the Royal Scots began arriving at Leith Station. From there they were taken to Dalmeny Street where the home of the battalion became a mortuary for its dead. Relatives of the victims were prevented from opening the coffins because many of the bodies were so severely mangled and disfigured. On 24 May the funeral of one hundred men took place. Survivors of the crash had already returned from Liverpool and took part in the burial of their friends and comrades and many thousands of residents of Leith and the surrounding areas lined the streets to pay their respects. Leith essentially closed for a day of mourning. Despite the drill hall being only half a mile from Rosebank Cemetery where the coffins were to be laid in a mass grave, it took several hours to make the journey. Today a memorial to the men marks the site of the grave and there are further memorials near the site of the crash. The former drill hall itself is currently an arts and cultural venue, acting once again as a hub for the surrounding community, but it also remains the most poignant reminder of the many men who did not return to Leith and the impact their loss had on the locality.

Supplying the Front

WOMEN AT WAR
Imperial War Museum, London

With high numbers of men leaving their jobs across Scotland to take part in the war, first as volunteers and then as conscripts following the Military Service Act in 1916, there was a critical need to replace them in the workforce. As a result of this, women were employed on a scale never before seen, with at least one million of them joining the British workforce over the course of the war. In addition to continuing in more traditional roles such as nursing, many women found employment in industries and agriculture. For example, by the end of the war, more than 30,000 women were employed in the munitions industry within Scotland. Many women also volunteered for service overseas, where they served as doctors, nurses, drivers and clerical assistants. Although many working women enjoyed their new financial independence and the opportunities they were now being given, life was not always easy and the work could often be dangerous. After the war, the efforts they had put in during the conflict gave considerable strength to the cause of women's suffrage within Britain, as the work they had carried out had shown they were capable of far more than society traditionally permitted.

The First World War made a huge impact on manufacturing and industry in Scotland and the sheer scale of the conflict posed titanic logistical challenges. Soldiers needed equipment, ships needed fuel and millions of guns, large and small, needed ammunition. The challenge was not only to manufacture the necessary supplies and equipment but also to move them in enormous quantities across land and sea to wherever they were required. By 1914 Scotland was already a heavily industrialised nation but this proved insufficient for the demands of war. New industries appeared across the country especially to produce products previously sourced from abroad. The Ministry of Munitions was established in 1915 to manage the vast industrial effort required to support the war and in response to a shortage of artillery shells on the front lines. This new arm of government enabled centralised and improved industrial efficiency and allocated funding to the construction of new facilities and the expansion of existing ones. Major industrial figures were involved in advising the ministry and some of them were able to expand and diversify their own operations to aid the war effort, with substantial government support. The scale of these industries ranged from vast purpose-built complexes such as the cordite factories at Gretna on the Solway coast, to small cottage industries. All of these industries required additional labour and as many of the men of working age had volunteered for military service or later in the war were conscripted, women entered the workforce in huge numbers. Expanding industries and their increasingly large labour forces would drastically change the nature of Scotland and Scottish society. Although the physical legacy of the industry of war has in many places been lost in the intervening century some locations do survive as a testament to the war effort.

Scotland's largest contribution was probably its shipbuilding industry centred on the shipyards of the Clyde. Long known for the quality of their work and relatively safe from German attack, at the outbreak of war three of the largest shipyards were officially designated as naval dockyards, including

FORT MATILDA ↘
National Archives, Kew

Fort Matilda in Greenock. The site of the coast artillery battery at [1] is now an office building. At [2], which was a torpedo factory, no buildings are visible on the map as the area was classified. The blue-hatched line denoting barbed wire, a trench and two blockhouses (or pillboxes) provided defence from the west. Areas [3] and [4] are barracks for the 3rd Battalion Royal Scots Fusiliers. At [5] is the submarine mining station, which was known as HMS *Dalriada*.

A NEW TOWN →
RCAHMS

An aerial view of Union Road and Annan Road. At the start of the war, to cope with the munitions shortages, an extensive cordite factory was built along the Solway shore. The town of Gretna was rapidly constructed alongside this to house and entertain the factory workers and families.

John Brown's at Clydebank, Fairfield's in Govan and William Beardmore's at Dalmuir. In total, almost fifty shipyards of various sizes on the Clyde alone were involved in the war effort. Brown's, Fairfield's and Beardmore's built four battle-cruisers, ten light cruisers, two aircraft carriers, twenty-nine submarines and eighty-five destroyers between them, alongside numerous other military and mercantile vessels. By the close of the conflict the Clyde shipyards had built around 451 warships and almost 600 other vessels for the Royal Navy as well as many civilian and merchant vessels. To maintain wartime rates of production skilled shipyard workers were not allowed to volunteer for the forces and were even exempted from conscription when it was introduced in 1916. Sadly little remains today of the enormous shipbuilding industry on the Clyde other than one prominent reminder, the monumental Titan Crane that was built at John Brown's Clydebank yard in 1907 and which was vital to its operations during the war.

With the enormous volume of ammunition being consumed on the battlefronts Scotland played a significant role in supplying munitions, a key part of the war effort. In the late nineteenth century Alfred Nobel had established a dynamite factory at Ardeer in Ayrshire, which continued in use throughout the war. Near the Scottish border on the Solway coast a vast new cordite factory at its peak required accommodation to house a workforce of 14,000 men and women. This led to the construction of an entire new town, Gretna in Dumfries and Galloway. The Ordnance Depot beside the Forth at Stirling began operating at the end of the nineteenth century but expanded substantially during the war years and two vast naval ammunition stores were built downriver at Bandeath and Crombie. At Eldon Street in Greenock, near Glasgow, a factory opened just before the war to design and manufacture torpedoes, which were then tested in Loch Long. Shipyards and other heavy industries diversified into other areas of production. The North British Locomotive Company built two new factories producing artillery shells

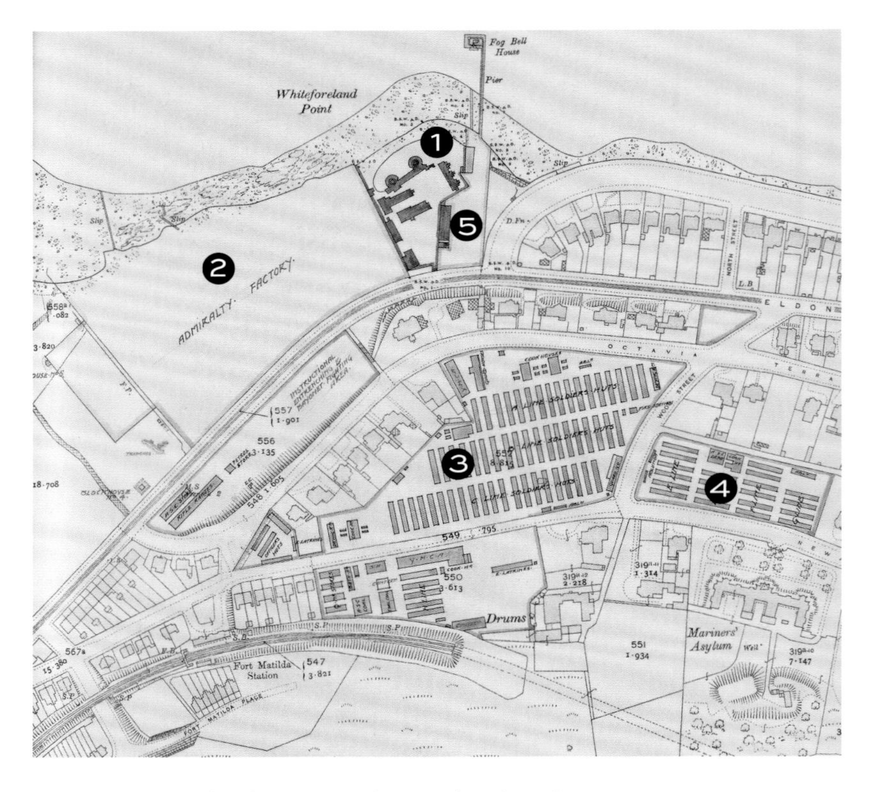

and mines. Scotland is not now known for aircraft construction but at Dalmuir in West Dunbartonshire and Inchinnan in Renfrewshire, the Beardmore Company began building both fixed-wing aircraft (land and seaplanes) and airships, completing more than 500 in total by 1918. In addition to Beardmore and other factories on the Clyde, aircraft were also built in Alloa in Clackmannanshire. Even Aberdeen, which did not have an aerodrome at that time, sent completed aircraft south by rail. Towards the end of the war, John Brown's shipyard began constructing tanks and the newly built Arrol-Johnston factory at Dumfries almost immediately transferred from car production to the construction of aircraft engines.

Other industries in Scotland enjoyed a boom period as a result of the demands of war. Coal was still the fuel of industry and empire. Scottish coalfields supplied tens of millions of tons each year during the war to shipping, industry and the

railways. Dundee's jute industry supplied, among other items, sandbags for the army, vital in trench warfare and needed at a rate of several million per month at times during the conflict. The Scottish steel industry, which was already producing over twenty per cent of the steel output in Britain at the start of the war, doubled its production rate to around 2.5 million tons by the end of the conflict. The vast industrial changes taking place across Scotland would have been futile without suitable and effective transport. Indeed, logistical problems of keeping men supplied with front line essentials such as food and ammunition, while they were rapidly moving further away from the stores and depots as part of an attempted offensive (even for an advance of only a few miles) were a major factor in the relatively static nature of warfare on the Western Front for many years. Improvements in supplying the British and French forces by 1917 helped to break the deadlock.

Although motor vehicles were becoming a common sight around Britain by the start of the war, the main form of long-distance transport was still the vast network of railways built in the 1800s and which stretched for thousands of miles linking villages, towns and cities. The railways already connected existing major industries with major ports and provided the supply chain for the British forces overseas. They also carried most of the soldiers and sailors from their homes to training areas, barracks and, ultimately, to the front lines. Where industries sprang up as part of the war effort, new connections to the existing railway network would also appear, as at Gretna. Goods would be taken from the industrial areas of Scotland to the channel ports of southern England for transfer

TITAN CRANE
Andrew Lee

The enormous Titan Crane played a crucial part in the war effort. The 150 foot high structure was the world's first electrically powered cantilever crane. It was built at John Brown's Shipyard at Clydebank in 1907 and was used for lifting heavy engineering parts, such as boilers and gun mountings. Over the course of the war John Brown's built a total of forty-seven warships and later in the war were also building other items such as tanks. Today the Titan Crane is open as a visitor attraction, one of the last reminders of this once mighty industry.

to France. Meanwhile, a steady stream of naval personnel made long journeys north to the base at Rosyth and even longer trips onward to Caithness for seaborne transfer to the Grand Fleet in Scapa Flow. In order to ensure the smooth and effective running of the railways and to maintain their vital supply role, the entire industry was placed under state control at the outbreak of war.

The immense requirement for supplies led to a massive transfer of materials from overseas to Britain. Raw materials, finished products and food arrived particularly from the United States and Canada. Convoys were instituted to protect incoming shipping against German U-boat attack. Supplies of food and equipment entered through all the major ports on the west coast, especially Glasgow. Towards the end of the war tens of thousands of American mines were delivered to ports near Fort William in the Highland estuaries at Corpach and Kyle of Lochalsh from where they were transferred to Inverness and Invergordon by train for use in the North Sea Mine Barrage.

The industrial efforts and activities during the war would have a profound impact on society. To fill vacancies in vital jobs left by men joining the military, not only did women enter the workforce but roles previously considered only suitable for skilled tradesmen began to be carried out by unskilled labour. Prisoners of war were deployed to work in agriculture, forestry and mining. Many of these transformative influences only grew stronger after the war ended. People who made up the new workforce were reluctant to return to their proscribed and limited pre-war roles in society. Women significantly campaigned for voting rights and maintained demands for equality at home and in the workplace. There was also friction as returning soldiers looked to reclaim their old lives and workers with new political power challenged industrial leaders. Nevertheless, for a while people began to hope for a golden age for industry in Scotland. They could not anticipate that the recessions of the 1920s and the resurgence of a militaristic Germany in the 1930s would soon destroy any dreams of a better world.

SEAPLANES AT DALMUIR

Bruce/Leslie Collection, licensor SCRAN

Seaplanes under construction at William Beardmore's Dalmuir works. Beardmore made ships, submarines, tanks and artillery. William Beardmore was also a shareholder in the Arrol-Johnston motorcar factory in Dumfries where aircraft and aero-engines were made. This led to the construction of aircraft production facilities at Dalmuir. By the end of the war Beardmore's had produced almost 500 aircraft.

ARROL-JOHNSTON, DUMFRIES

RCAHMS

The Category B listed Arrol-Johnston works at Dumfries was built in 1913 and used for aircraft engine manufacture in the First World War. This view of the exterior shows the factory with the power station to the left. The building is of a style rare in Britain, emulating American pre-war industrial style.

TROOPS ON THE MOVE
National Museums of Scotland, licensor SCRAN

Troops lined up on the platform at Huntly Station, Aberdeenshire, awaiting a train. Mass mobilisation of the armed forces put added demands on the railway network and infrastructure to transport the vast numbers of soldiers across the country to war.

AMMUNITION ON THE MOVE
National Museums of Scotland, licensor SCRAN

A substantial stockpile of artillery shells awaiting transport. The enormous requirements of materials for the war required an equally massive logistical effort, with railways and shipping operating around the clock to move equipment, vehicles, food, medicine and ammunition to and from manufacturing and production sites to depots and stores across the country, and onwards to the men and women serving abroad.

MAKERS OF MACHINES

Glasgow City Council, licensor SCRAN

Tanks and railway locomotives being built on adjacent production lines at the North British Locomotive Company works at Springburn. During the First World War, the North British Locomotive Company produced not only tanks but also shells of all sizes, shell forgings, portable pillboxes and sea mines. A large part of this work was undertaken by women. The company also manufactured aeroplanes, trench Howitzer carriages, military bridges, artificial limbs and machine tools as well as continuing to produce locomotive engines, some for specialised military use such as the movement of guns and ammunition.

1611
1611

Broken Bodies and Broken Minds

SPRINGBURN HOSPITAL

Glasgow City Council, licensor SCRAN

As existing hospitals were insufficient to cope with the war wounded, the directors of the North British Locomotive Company gave over the main part of their administration building to the Scottish branch of the British Red Cross. The resulting Springburn Hospital had 400 beds, an operating theatre, x-ray room as well as recreation areas, sitting rooms, bedrooms and kitchen accommodation. The hospital, one of three military hospitals in the area, opened for the reception of patients on 24 December 1914 and remained open throughout the war. The work required to modify the building for use as a hospital was extensive and the North British Locomotive Company met all the costs involved. By the time the hospital closed, more than 8,000 patients had been treated there. The public donated bedding and other comforts, and the Red Cross booklet of 1915 states that for the sum of £50 a donor could name a bed. Patients not confined to bed wore distinctive blue suits with red ties.

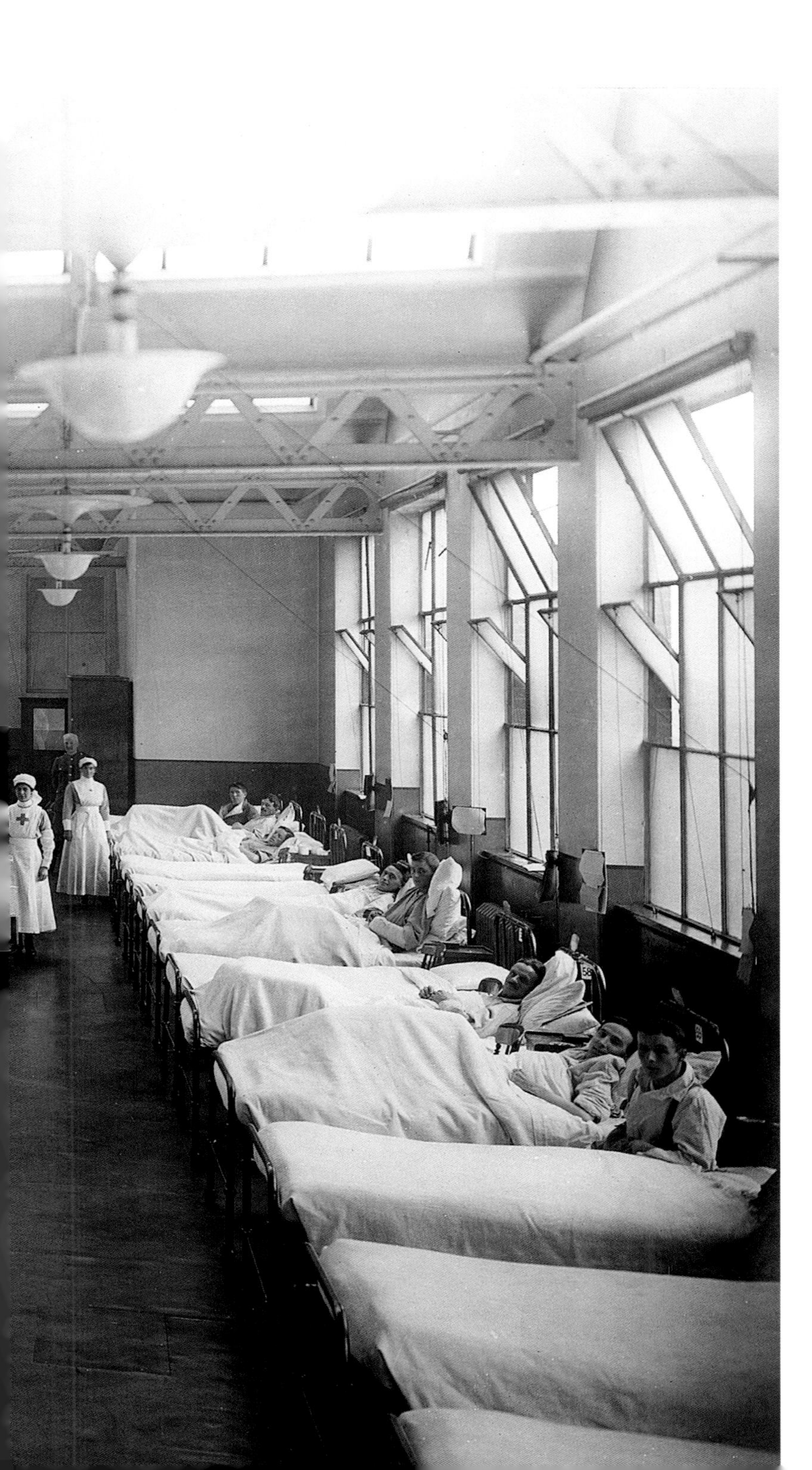

The scale of the First World War was unprecedented and it is hardly surprising that the number of casualties was so high. During major offensives the casualty rate soared to thousands every day. War on such an industrial scale meant enormous levels of injury and illness among combatants. It was a fact of daily life that a steady stream of men would be withdrawn from the front line to receive treatment for many different conditions. These included combat injuries from enemy snipers, artillery fire and gas attacks; illnesses such as trench foot, dysentery, trench fever, tetanus and cholera; and psychological trauma or post-traumatic stress disorder known at the time as shell shock. In the British Army the treatment of the wounded and sick was the responsibility of the Royal Army Medical Corps. In a similar manner to the carefully planned approach, which ensured that men, machinery and supplies reached the front line, a system was developed to bring the wounded and sick out of the line for treatment. This system was known as the Chain of Evacuation and it stretched from the violent heart of the battlefields right back to the cities, towns and villages of Scotland.

At the outbreak of war there were around 7,000 beds at military hospitals in Britain and less than a third of these were being used. In Scotland there were no military hospitals of any significant size although a naval hospital did exist at Butlaw in South Queensferry to serve the fleet based at Rosyth. All the regimental depots had their own small hospitals, either within the barracks, as at the Maryhill Barracks in Glasgow and the Cameron Barracks in Inverness, or nearby such as Castlehill Barracks in Aberdeen. By November 1918 the total number of beds available to the army had reached 364,133, of which 24,291 were in Scotland. Hospitals ranged from substantial facilities capable of holding several thousand cases down to those providing beds for only a few convalescing soldiers at any one time. Creating the extra capacity required was achieved through a variety of methods including active fundraising spread across Scotland under the jurisdiction of Scottish

WORKERS REMEMBERED
RCAHMS

The Category A listed administration block of the former North British Locomotive Company. A plaque inside the building commemorates its wartime use and another lists the names of the 300 workers who died in the conflict. More than 3,000 employees from the company served in the war. The chairman, Sir William Lorimer, unveiled the plaque on 24 March 1921. Three magnificent stained glass windows by William Meikle & Sons further commemorate the sacrifice of the Springburn workers. The building is now a business centre.

Command, which was one of nine command divisions of the Royal Army Medical Corps. Military hospitals were therefore directly connected to specific military facilities such as regimental depots and naval bases. Although expanded during the war each of these medical centres remained relatively small. New military hospitals were built as part of recently developed bases, such as in the Highlands at Cromarty and Invergordon. In total, eighteen military hospitals operated in Scotland during the First World War. There were also three Territorial Force general hospitals established at Aberdeen, Edinburgh and Glasgow. In Aberdeen, the hospital was spread across the buildings of four different schools and connected to the city poorhouse and could accommodate almost 1,500 casualties at any one time.

Reception hospitals were often the first stop in Scotland for arriving casualties or the final stop before soldiers were returned to the front line. They were used to process less severe casualties before they were transferred to other hospitals for further treatment. Scotland had five reception hospitals: two in Ayrshire, at Turnberry in the same building as the officers' mess for the air station and at Camlarg House, Dalmellington; Lindores Manor (now a hotel) in Greenock near Glasgow; Invergordon in the eastern Highlands; and one on the island of Inchkeith.

In order to deal with the substantial number of casualties requiring treatment and recovery time, the Royal Army Medical Corps requisitioned civilian hospitals and asylums. These war hospitals provided several thousand available beds for treatment. In particular, the recently constructed 'lunatic asylums' as they were then called, were well equipped and had modern facilities. Bangour Village Hospital, which opened in 1906, became the Edinburgh War Hospital with a capacity of over 2,600 beds. In addition to the large asylums, smaller war hospitals were accommodated in poorhouses such as those at Leith in Edinburgh, Dundee and Crookston in Glasgow. By far the highest numbers of hospitals during the war were civilian

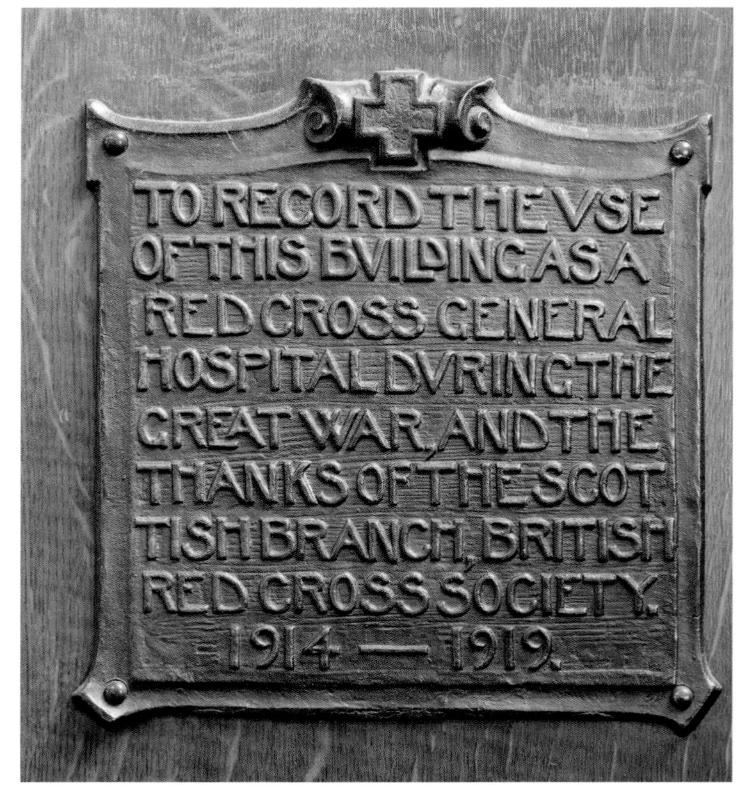

MILITARY HOSPITAL OF EDINBURGH CASTLE ↑
Historic Scotland, Edinburgh

Military hospitals were directly connected to military facilities, such as regimental depots and naval bases. Some were already in place before the war and others underwent significant expansion during the conflict. An ordnance store at Edinburgh Castle was first converted into a hospital in 1897 and was used again during the war. The hospital dealt with over one hundred German casualties after the sinking of the German battleship SMS *Blucher* at the battle of Dogger Bank on 24 January 1915, the largest naval battle of the war at that time.

MILITARY HOSPITAL OF EDINBURGH CASTLE ↑
Lothian Health Services Archive, licensor SCRAN

Staff and patients outside the military hospital of Edinburgh Castle. This building now houses part of the National War Museum.

WOODEND HOSPITAL IN ABERDEEN ↓
Robert Gordon University, licensor SCRAN

Woodend Hospital in Aberdeen formed part of the 1st Scottish General Hospital during the war.

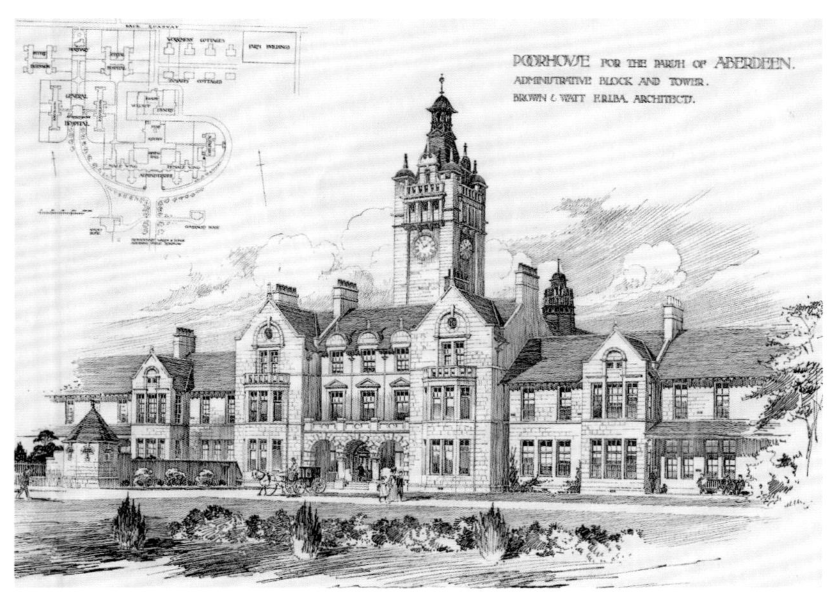

and auxiliary hospitals. Existing civilian hospitals allocated some of their beds for military casualties. Many smaller hospitals staffed by volunteers were created and run by established aid organisations such as the British Red Cross, alongside many smaller charities and volunteer organisations created specifically to help. Local auxiliary hospitals were established in hotels, village halls and country houses across Scotland ranging in capacity from just a few beds to several hundred. Despite the inherently inefficient nature of some of the very smallest auxiliary hospitals, they were felt to be of significant value, as described by one medical officer: 'We do not wish to close down, as these hospitals do a good work in keeping alive the people's interest in the war and we feel that if for no other reason than this, it would be unwise to remove the only object-lesson which an isolated country district like this can possibly have of the existence of our national struggle.'

Although far from the front lines hospitals gave staff working in them a more graphic, brutal and realistic portrayal of the reality of the war, far removed from state-controlled propaganda. Effie Day, a volunteer nurse at Bangour near Edinburgh, described the day she started there:

I had wanted to be a volunteer nurse from the day that war broke out in 1914, but had to wait until my eighteenth birthday. Although I was enthusiastic, I had absolutely no idea what awaited me at Bangour and what I saw on that first day made me want to run straight home to Edinburgh. I was told to take up duties in a medical ward, but even there the suffering was terrible to see. There were young

AUXILIARY HOSPITALS
National Museums of Scotland, licensor SCRAN

Patients at Whitehill Auxiliary Hospital near Carrington, Midlothian. In an attempt to cheer up the injured soldiers, staff at the hospital have tried to get their patients into a festive mood by putting up decorations. As wounded servicemen began to arrive back in great numbers, the British Red Cross and other organisations established auxiliary hospitals to ease pressure on the larger military hospitals. The hospitals varied greatly in size and were to be found in town halls, recreation halls, schools, and in small and large private houses, such as this A-listed Jacobean mansion at Whitehill. Whitehill remained in use as a hospital from 1914 until 1998.

ROSEBERY CUP
British Red Cross, SCRAN

The British Red Cross Society was active both at home and abroad during the war. Here, members of the Lothian detachment are competing in an official contest, the Roseberry Cup, intended to test their skills.

RECEPTION HOSPITALS
RCAHMS

Turnberry Hotel, Ayrshire, was Scotland's first resort hotel. During the war the building housed a reception hospital and the officers' mess for Turnberry air station. The luxury resort opened in 1906 as the Turnberry Station Hotel and was commandeered for use during both world wars. The Category B listed building remains in use as a hotel today.

boys who had been blinded by mustard gas in the trenches in Belgium. Others were suffering from dysentery, malaria and even black water fever.

The horrific dangers of the front line led to swift medical advances during the war. Great strides were made in treatment, from the emergency efforts on the front lines right through to the long-term recovery of the wounded. Attempts to prevent the spread of infection and disease, despite difficult conditions, progressed steadily. Treatment and recovery improved in the hospitals in France and Britain. Reconstructive plastic surgery, although in its infancy, allowed some semblance of normality for disfigured soldiers whose wounds a few years earlier would have killed them. Orthopaedic advances repaired damaged skeletons while improved prosthetics replaced missing limbs. Despite this, many who spent time in the hospitals around Scotland and those who cared for them would live with the physical and mental pain of their experiences for the rest of their lives.

Craiglockhart Hospital

CRAIGLOCKHART HOSPITAL
The Owen Estate, licensor SCRAN

Staff gathered outside the Craiglockhart War Hospital. The hospital was established to treat neurasthenia or 'shell shock', a psychological illness, which today is recognised as post-traumatic stress disorder. The hospital operated for a number of years, although it faced a constant battle to do so, as many of the senior military and medical staff of the army simply refused to believe that shell shock was truly an illness at all, instead believing the victims were simply cowards. Although the hospital existed to treat the mental suffering of its patients, it was not necessarily the mercy it appeared, as the goal was to aid their recovery so they could be returned to the same front lines that had damaged them in the first place. The patients treated at Craiglockhart were all officers, who as a group suffered an unusually high rate of shell shock during the war, and among the patients treated there during the war were some of the greatest war poets, including Robert Graves, Wilfred Owen and Siegfried Sassoon.

The Craiglockhart Hydropathic Hospital was opened in 1880 but had fallen out of use when the War Office requisitioned it in 1916 as a war hospital for officers. Initially under the command of Major William Bryce the hospital was established specifically to treat psychological disorders, most notably the treatment of shell shock. Shell shock would now be considered a post-traumatic stress disorder caused by the horrors of life on the front lines of the war. Although a psychological disorder, shell shock could manifest in physical symptoms, ranging from nervous tics, dizziness and cramps to blindness, deafness and paralysis. Around 80,000 soldiers in the British Army had been treated for shell shock by the end of the war. According to a survey in 1917, a particularly high number of officers suffered from shell shock: at the front the ratio of officers to men was around one in thirty, yet among patients being treated for shell shock the ratio of officers to men was one in six. Despite medical recognition of their suffering, society at large was often far less sympathetic to victims of shell shock than the doctors who were treating them. Attitudes to the illness were often uncompromising among some ranks of the military and even the more traditional medical professionals.

Establishing Craiglockhart as a military hospital was an attempt to find new ways to treat victims. This was not primarily for humane reasons but to get the wounded well enough to return to the fighting that had caused their trauma in the first place. The two doctors deputed to Major Bryce at the hospital were Arthur Brock, an Edinburgh man who had worked with similar conditions before the war and William Rivers. Founder of the British Journal of Psychology in 1908, Rivers developed what became known as the 'talking cure'. He encouraged soldiers to discuss their experiences, rather than to repress them and through this reach an acceptance that their experiences would not be something they could force themselves to forget. As he stated in a paper to the Royal Society of Medicine in December 1917:

It is natural to thrust aside painful memories just as

it is natural to avoid dangerous or horrible scenes in actuality, and this natural tendency to banish the distressing or the horrible is especially pronounced in those whose powers of resistance have been lowered by the long-continued strains of trench-life, the shock of shell-explosion, or other catastrophe of war.

The methods used by Rivers appear to have been relatively effective in treating victims of shell shock, but it was a slow process. Although discussing their experiences helped patients many still suffered months and even years of psychological trauma. Siegfried Sassoon who was treated at Craiglockhart by Rivers gave a version of the treatment in his semi-autobiographical novel *Sherston's Progress*:

In the daytime, sitting in a sunny room, a man could discuss his psycho-neurotic symptoms with his doctor, who could diagnose phobias and conflicts and formulate them into scientific terminology. Significant dreams could be noted down, and Rivers could try to remove repressions. But by night each man was back in his doomed sector of horror-stricken Front Line, where the panic and stampede of some ghastly experience was re-enacted among the livid faces of the dead. No doctor could save him then, when he became the lonely victim of his dream disasters and delusions.

Sassoon was not suffering from shell shock, instead he had been sent to Craiglockhart at the behest of his friend Robert Graves, himself a former patient, to escape a court martial after his written objections and criticism of the war were presented to parliament. Wilfred Owen was also at Craiglockhart and he and Sassoon became close friends. Both wrote some of their finest works there. Craiglockhart has long since ceased to be a hospital but remains as a testament to those victims of wartime psychological trauma and to the men and women who treated them with compassion in the face of opposition and even hostility, perhaps best described by Sassoon himself in his poem *Survivors*, written at the hospital:

SIEGFRIED SASSOON
National Portrait Gallery, London

The poet and author Siegfried Sassoon was treated at Craiglockhart in 1917, after writing his 'Declaration against the War', which was subsequently read out in parliament to considerable anger. His friend Robert Graves convinced the authorities to send him to Craiglockhart for treatment as a neurasthenia victim rather than to a court martial. Sassoon wrote a great deal about his time at the hospital, which he nicknamed 'Dottyville'.

No doubt they'll soon get well; the shock and strain
Have caused their stammering, disconnected talk.
Of course they're 'longing to go out again,' –
These boys with old, scared faces, learning to walk.
They'll soon forget their haunted nights; their cowed
Subjection to the ghosts of friends who died, –
Their dreams that drip with murder; and they'll be proud
Of glorious war that shatter'd all their pride...
Men who went out to battle, grim and glad;
Children, with eyes that hate you, broken and mad.

CRAIGLOCKHART HOSPITAL
Edinburgh Napier University

The Craiglockhart Hydropathic Hospital was built by Peddie & Kinnear architects between 1878-80. It was originally designed to give the appearance of a lavish hydropathic hotel establishment, for paying patients, but it had fallen out of use by the time it was requisitioned as a war hospital for officers in 1916.

Prisoners of War

PRISONERS AT WORK
British Geological Survey/NERC, licensor SCRAN

Prisoners of war, photographed on the island of Raasay where they were deployed to work in the iron mine. Many prisoners of war were given some form of employment during their time in captivity, for which they received a small wage, and this was permitted under the legal conventions governing their treatment. As a result, prisoners of war from the enemy nations could be found working in agriculture, construction, forestry and industry across Scotland. Construction of the iron mine on Raasay was begun in 1911, following the purchase of the island by William Baird and Company for the purpose. The mine was only completed as the war broke out, and as all thirty-six miners left the island to join up, the mine was forced to close almost as soon as it was finished. However, as the war progressed and the need for iron grew, it was decided in 1916 to use prisoners to work the mine. The prisoners on the island had the luxury of living in the cottages, which had been built for the use of the miners before they left.

It was not only wounded soldiers who were returned to Britain but also captured enemy soldiers. In 1914 relatively few prisoners were brought to Scotland but as the war changed into more familiar forms of attack and counter attack between entrenched enemies, the number of captives increased. In the years before the outbreak of the First World War the Hague Convention and the Geneva Convention had ratified rules for the conduct of war, including the treatment of enemy prisoners, but it is unlikely that anyone anticipated the number of prisoners that would be taken during the First World War. By the end of 1914, there were over 1.3 million prisoners being held in captivity by various nations.

The level of accommodation required to cope with the increasing volume of prisoners required first the utilisation of existing buildings and subsequently the rapid construction of camps. In the early months of the war many camps were overcrowded and reports of the maltreatment of captives came from all sides, although much of this proved to be unfounded. To counter the accusations, observers from neutral nations such as the United States together with the British Red Cross monitored the conduct of the camps.

In Scotland the very first captives of the war were held at existing military facilities in Edinburgh Castle and Fort George near Inverness. By the end of 1914, thirteen prisoner of war camps had been created in Britain, including one in Scotland at Stobs Camp near Hawick, which became the headquarters of the prisoner of war camp system in Scotland. As the war progressed the number of camps continued to grow. By the close of 1915 there were two major camps in Scotland; the number grew to eight in 1916 and fourteen in 1917. Figures from various sources differ but by the end of hostilities there were between twenty-five and thirty-nine camps in Scotland holding many thousands of prisoners.

With certain restrictions enemy prisoners could be used for manual labour and this often influenced the location of the camps and the accommodation required. On the island of Raasay prisoners were

THE PRISON AT STOBS
Imperial War Museum, London

This image shows the extensive prisoner of war camp at Stobs, near Hawick. This was the headquarters of the prisoner of war system within Scotland, and as such it was by far the largest of the sites. The long wooden huts, which housed the prisoners, can be seen stretching across the slope, and one of these huts still survives at the site today. The pool in the foreground of the image is listed as a bathing pond on the Ordnance Survey's 3rd edition map of the area, a prospect that would no doubt be rather daunting in the depths of a Scottish winter.

put to work in the iron mine from 1916 because the former miners had joined up for the war. The prisoners were housed in the miners' cottages. At Kinlochleven and Caolas-na-Con, not far from Fort William, prisoners were employed in a variety of tasks connected to smelting operations, including the construction of the first road to the village along the shore of Loch Leven. Auchterarder was the headquarters for twelve prisons across Perthshire and Angus housing a large number of prisoners. At Loch Doon in Ayrshire prisoners assisted in the construction of the aerial gunnery school. Other detainees built dams for civilian water supplies in Beecraigs in West Lothian as well as in Perthshire. The captive men also built hospital facilities including those at Hairmyres in East Kilbride, Lanarkshire. The use of prisoners for building work at Rosyth naval base and Bandeath naval armaments depot – both on the Firth of Forth – may well have contravened the regulations which did not permit captured soldiers to be used in any activity that aided the enemy war effort.

Although prison life was undoubtedly safer than for their countrymen in the battle lines, some never returned home. At least two prisoners died at Kinlochleven, one of whom was shot attempting to escape, while eight succumbed to an outbreak of the deadly Spanish Flu in their camp at Braemore in the Highlands in February 1919. Nevertheless, most of the 250,000 prisoners held in Britain were eventually repatriated and their temporary homes disappeared from view, but the traces of those homes can still be found across Scotland.

Stobs Camp

STOBS FROM THE AIR
RCAHMS

This aerial view shows the extensive remains of the former training and prisoner of war camp at Stobs. The roadways and rectangular features at [1] are the remains of the prisoner of war camp, which can be seen on the previous page, with the building visible at [2] the last surviving example on the site of the prisoner of war huts. The features visible at [3] are the remains of the training camp on the site, which remained in use through the Second World War, when further construction occurred, such as the blastproof ammunition storage, the remains of which are clearly visible at [4]. In the landscape around the camp further indications of its history can be seen, including the remains of training trenches and traces of the purpose built station for the camp at Acreknowe Farm.

In 1902 the Stobs Estate put 10,000 acres of land south of Hawick up for sale. It was promptly bought by the War Office to establish a new training camp for the volunteer rifle regiments and later the territorial battalions. Work began on site in 1903 with the construction of a dedicated railway connection for the camp at Acreknowe Farm and other buildings including an officers' mess. As the camp was only intended for summer use no fixed accommodation was built, instead, trainees camped in tents. Nonetheless, Stobs saw heavy use with 20,000 men using the new camp in the first summer of its operation. With the outbreak of war, Stobs would become even busier.

When war was declared in August 1914, the territorial battalions camping at Stobs for their summer manoeuvres were immediately mobilised but remained there until they could be deployed to their wartime postings. Meanwhile further territorial units arrived from other areas around the country and were later joined by the raw recruits called up by Lord Kitchener to make up his New Army. Soon the camp was unable to cope and men had to be billeted in nearby Hawick in whatever buildings the army could requisition. Throughout the war men travelled to Stobs from all over Britain to train for active service. Evidence of the training areas, a network of trenches and the firing ranges that were used to prepare the troops for the front lines, can still be seen. New facilities such as huts for the men and a hospital were constructed to support mobilisation. It seems that life at Stobs was no picnic for the men. One soldier described it as 'a dreary, cheerless place...a damnable disgrace...simply call it Hell'.

As well as being a crucial training ground, Stobs became the headquarters of the prisoner of war camp system in Scotland. Wooden huts were built to house the growing number of captive enemy troops. Some were then assigned to other satellite camps around the country. Life for the prisoners of war at Stobs was in many ways more pleasant than for the army troops training beside them. Prisoners were provided with a school, an extensive library and their own hospital, as well as accommodation

STOBS CAMP, HAWICK ↓
National Library of Scotland, Edinburgh

This Ordnance Survey Map of Roxburghshire (1:2,500) from 1917 shows the extent of the camp at Stobs by that time.

GERMAN PRISONERS OF WAR →
Imperial War Museum, London

Stobs played an important role as the headquarters of the prisoner of war camp system in Scotland. Life for the prisoners at Stobs was in many ways more pleasant than for those undertaking military training as the prisoners had their own school, an extensive library, a hospital and accommodation huts. Prisoners who had been craftsmen before the war created elaborate items, which they sold to locals and visitors.

TRAINING AT STOBS CAMP ↘
Ian Lowes Collection

Men travelled to Stobs from all over the world to train for active service and evidence of the training areas can still be seen, with a network of training trenches and firing ranges that were used to prepare the troops for the front lines. New facilities and huts for the men and a hospital were constructed to support the training efforts.

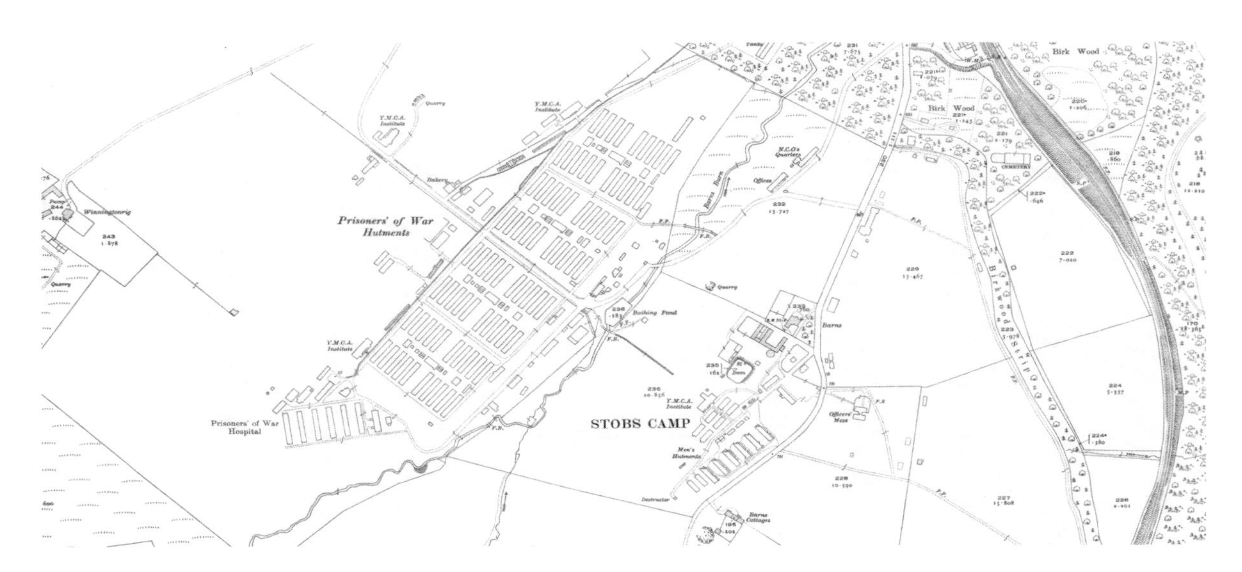

huts. Some of the prisoners formed an orchestra with donated instruments and the camp even had its own newspaper. Prisoners who had been craftsmen before the war took to creating elaborate items, which they would sell locally and to visitors. One British soldier wrote in 1916, 'We have five thousand German prisoners here and they have a better time of it than us.'

In addition to the military prisoners, many civilians were imprisoned at Stobs. The day after Britain declared war the government passed the Aliens' Restriction Act. This was intended to restrict the movement of spies through measures such as registration, relocation and imprisonment of Germans and Austrians suspected of being a risk to the country. While it may well have hindered the operations of enemy agents, it was undoubtedly mostly innocent people who found themselves suffering as a result of its draconian measures. By 1916, there were more than 2,000 civilians imprisoned at Stobs alone, with many more in other camps around Britain. Life for the civilian internees at Stobs was good in comparison to many of the camps, and they do not appear to have held any real resentment towards the guards holding them there, but it would be inaccurate to suggest it was happy. The very nature of their imprisonment placed a great mental strain on the prisoners, and some of them did not survive the war. The people held within had been the victims of hysterical anti-German sentiment brought on by the war, and they and their families suffered as result.

Throughout the conflict, many thousands of British troops, enemy prisoners of war and civilian internees would pass through Stobs. The camp was occupied again during the Second World War and was one of the accommodation camps used by the men of the Polish Army who had fought alongside the British Army before they were disbanded in 1947. Much of the site has since been cleared away but some tell-tale signs survive today of the vast settlement which once existed here. One of the huts occupied by the prisoners is still standing, a unique survival in Scotland, and there are further buildings to be found in the soldier's training camp, along with the training areas themselves, where faint traces of ditches in which so many thousands of young soldiers learned to fight can just be seen. In the small cemetery are the remains of a cairn memorial placed to commemorate forty-five prisoners who did not survive to return home.

Rauchen
Werkstätte STOBS.

Counting the Cost

THE SCUTTLING OF THE GERMAN HIGH SEAS FLEET
Orkney Islands Council, licensor SCRAN

Following the Armistice, the German High Seas Fleet was surrendered and detained, initially in the Forth and then within Scapa Flow. Several months later, as the peace negotiations drew to a close, the German commander, Admiral Ludwig von Reuter, was increasingly concerned about the fate of the ships in Allied hands and chose to take action. On 21 June 1919, after the majority of the Royal Navy vessels guarding the fleet had left the harbour to train, Von Reuter gave the order to scuttle the fleet. Within hours, fifty-two of the ships had sunk and nine Germans had been killed by mistake in the confusion. Many of the wrecks were salvaged after the war, but seven survive today on the seabed of Scapa Flow, three battleships, three cruisers and a mine-layer. They are protected as scheduled monuments and are a popular spot for divers.

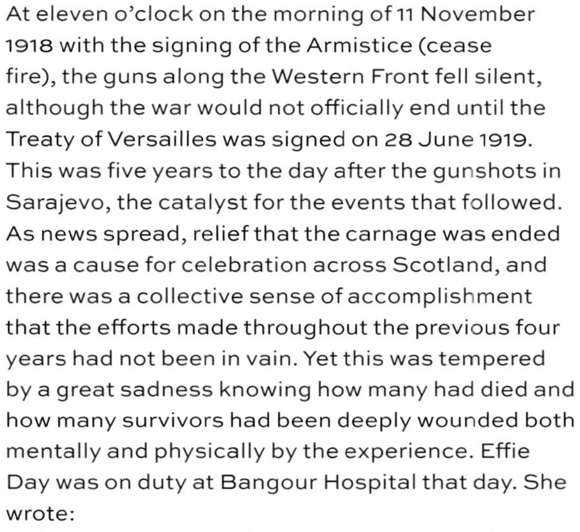

At eleven o'clock on the morning of 11 November 1918 with the signing of the Armistice (cease fire), the guns along the Western Front fell silent, although the war would not officially end until the Treaty of Versailles was signed on 28 June 1919. This was five years to the day after the gunshots in Sarajevo, the catalyst for the events that followed. As news spread, relief that the carnage was ended was a cause for celebration across Scotland, and there was a collective sense of accomplishment that the efforts made throughout the previous four years had not been in vain. Yet this was tempered by a great sadness knowing how many had died and how many survivors had been deeply wounded both mentally and physically by the experience. Effie Day was on duty at Bangour Hospital that day. She wrote:

At last in 1918 the terrible war drew to an end and on the morning of 11th November the lady doctor in charge of our ward made the wonderful announcement that we had all prayed for. The Armistice had been signed. We were at peace again. For a moment there was silence, then cheering the like of which I shall never forget. Soon we were all singing the songs that the war had made famous... Now we knew that none of our patients would have to face returning to the terrors of the trenches.

Those serving abroad shared similar feelings at the news that the fighting was to finish, although many had little chance to mark the occasion. For some of the forces it would still be many months before they were 'demobbed' and could finally return home. Alexander Jamieson of the Royal Scots Fusiliers was serving east of Ypres in early November as news of the Armistice spread:

We came back out of the line at a place called Vichte [in Flanders] and had gone to bed in a hayloft. Our sergeant came in shouting that the war was over. Everybody got up and went down into this wee village. The estaminet owner opened his pub and issued free drinks and then went back to bed. We were paraded at the usual time. We were made to do slope-arms by numbers till eleven o' clock. Then we were disbanded. That was the Armistice.

LYNESS CEMETERY
Historic Scotland, Edinburgh

The German graves within the Lyness Naval Cemetery include the nine sailors who were shot by mistake during the scuttling of the German High Seas Fleet at Scapa Flow in 1919.

IN MEMORIAM →
National Museums of Scotland, licensor SCRAN

An unveiling service at Auchtermuchty in Fife, 1919. Union Jacks shroud the war memorial; the flag is often placed over coffins of dead servicemen and women as a mark of respect.

BLOODY FRIDAY ↘
Glasgow Museums, licensor SCRAN

Bloody Friday riots on 31 January 1919 in George Square, Glasgow. More than 60,000 people went on strike and gathered to oppose new rules on working hours, and widespread fighting broke out between the strikers and the police. Soon after the British government had deployed thousands of troops, along with tanks, artillery and machine guns, to suppress the uprising.

Precise casualty figures for Scotland have never been established. A definitive figure has been impossible due to inaccurate records, the movements of soldiers between battalions and regiments and the vast numbers of missing soldiers whose remains were never recovered. The approximate figure is thought to be around 150,000 out of almost 700,000 Scots who served. The figure is one of the highest percentages by total population of any country involved in the conflict and around 1.5 per cent of the ten million dead around the globe. The scale of the loss was unprecedented. It is unlikely that there was anyone in Scotland who did not lose a friend, colleague or family member to the war. The battlefields of Loos, Arras, the Somme and Gallipoli, among many others, became the graves for tens of thousands of Scots alongside their allies as well as their enemies. Many thousands of men returned with injuries that would seriously affect them for the rest of their lives and in some cases wounded combatants died only months after the end of the war. Other lives were lost in tragic accidents on both sides of the conflict. The sinking of the HMS *Iolaire* and the scuttling of the German High Seas Fleet were just two incidents that added to the tragic toll of casualties in 1919, while at the same time Scottish soldiers were still on active service against Bolshevik revolutionaries in Russia. The war continued to directly impact on Scotland long after 11 November 1918.

Even before the war ended consideration was being given to suitable ways to remember the heroism, sacrifice and suffering of those involved in the conflict. Many veterans in particular did not wish to see their comrades remembered so far away from the front lines where they fell and many simply

TE DEUM. LAUDAMUS
COMMERCIAL HOTEL
MRS HARDIE

KITCHENER MEMORIAL ↘
Historic Scotland, Edinburgh

The Kitchener Memorial on Marwick Head, Orkney is a grand, square stone tower which was erected and paid for by the people of Orkney to commemorate Lord Kitchener and the crew of HMS *Hampshire*. The memorial overlooks the spot where on 5 June 1916 HMS *Hampshire* sank after striking a German mine.

FOCHABERS MEMORIAL →
Nick Haynes

The Fochabers and Bellie War Memorial. The positioning of this memorial within the designed landscape of Gordon Castle and the style in which it has been built have been carefully chosen to take advantage of the wider landscape to enhance the memorial.

ERSKINE HOSPITAL ↘
RCAHMS

Erskine House, now the Mar Hall Hotel, in Bishopton housed the Erskine Hospital both during and after the war. And, the work which began in this building continues today; as a charity, Erskine provides care and support for veterans across Scotland.

wanted their experiences consigned entirely to the past. In the end, memorials to the fallen and their accomplishments alongside the celebration of the victory that they had helped to achieve became an enormous undertaking. A national memorial to the Scottish fallen was established in Edinburgh Castle and this was complemented by many thousands of memorials across the country. Many memorials were simple, just a stone Celtic cross or pillar with a plaque listing the names of the men from the area who had been lost, yet they still have great poignancy. Other memorials were much more elaborate. On Dundee Law a towering granite structure stands over the town. It has a bronze brazier on top and a beacon is still lit to commemorate anniversaries such as the Armistice. In Coatbridge, North Lanarkshire the memorial is a large circular structure in the form of a classical arbour made of grey granite. Unusually, it was designed by a woman, Edith Burnet Hughes, a pioneering architect and the niece of the famed Scottish architect, J.J. Burnet. Other ways of memorialising the fallen and the victory were more functional, with public parks created, such as at Helensburgh on the Clyde and memorial halls like that at Fort Augustus, on the shore of Loch Ness.

Memorials were also built to recognise particular groups and individuals. At Lyness on Hoy the naval cemetery commemorates men from around the world buried there as well as the thousands lost at sea during the war. Amongst the graves of allied sailors are those of fourteen Germans, including those who died during the scuttling of the fleet. A number of industries chose to commemorate those men who left their jobs behind and never returned. The Caledonian Railway placed a bronze memorial plaque inside the main entrance to Glasgow Central Station, which listed 706 names. In Paisley, ceramic tiles with the names of former workers at the Royal Doulton factory were used in a memorial in Hawkhead Cemetery. At Marwick Head in Orkney, a great tower stands in commemoration of Lord Kitchener who was lost when HMS *Hampshire* sank off the coast in 1916.

In addition to the commemoration of the dead, considerable resources were needed to care for the survivors with long-term physical and psychological injuries. New charitable foundations such as the Royal British Legion and the Earl Haig Fund were established to raise funds to support returning veterans. In 1916, the Princess Louise Hospital for Limbless Sailors and Soldiers was established in Erskine House on the southern bank of the Clyde. The hospital treated around twenty per cent of the British veterans who returned from the front with disabling injuries. The Erskine Foundation continues its work with veterans across Scotland to this day. At Whitefoord House in Edinburgh the Lady Haig Poppy Factory was established in 1926 employing men who had been disabled to make poppies for Scotland. These small red flowers, so common on the battlefields of France and Belgium, have become a symbol of remembrance, not only of veterans of the First World War but also to commemorate the sacrifices made by all veterans in all conflicts.

SINKING OF SMS BAYERN
Imperial War Museum, London

The SMS *Bayern* sinks in Scapa Flow following the scuttling. This battleship was only a few years old when she sank, having only come into service in July 1916. In 1934 she became one of the many battleships, which were recovered during the enormous salvage operation on the fleet between the wars, although when she was being raised the four main gun turrets broke free and were left behind on the seabed, where they remain today.

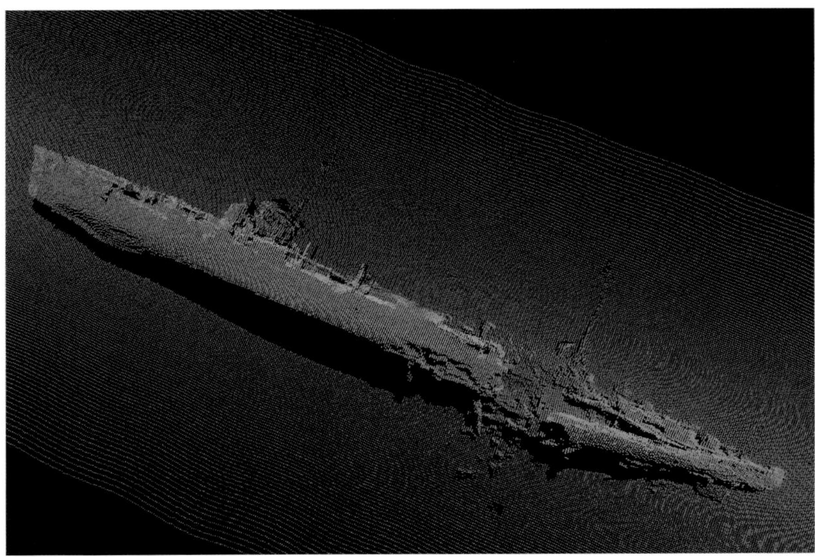

SEABED SCAN OF THE GERMAN LIGHT CRUISER SMS KOLN
ScapaMAP

A sonar scan of the wreck of the SMS *Koln* on the seabed of Scapa Flow. The SMS *Koln* is one of only seven ships from the German High Seas Fleet, which remain where they sank. As they had been scuttled in deeper water they could not be feasibly salvaged.

ON GUARD
National Museums of Scotland, licensor SCRAN

When it became apparent that the German ships were being scuttled, attempts were made to navigate the sinking ships into shallower water by the shoreline, where they could be easily recovered. This destroyer was successfully beached before she could sink, and is under guard by three soldiers shortly afterwards.

The Scottish National War Memorial

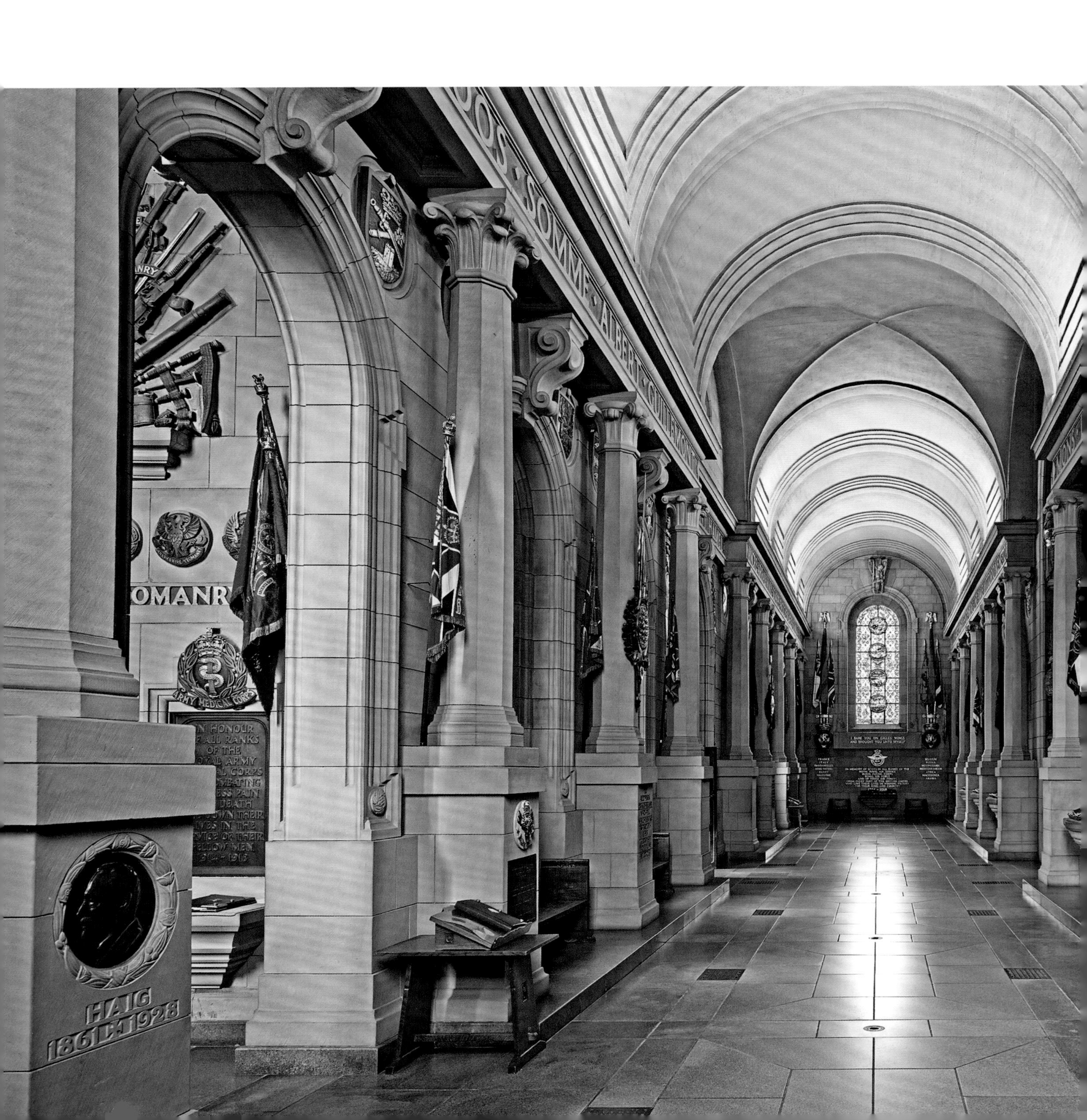

THE SCOTTISH NATIONAL WAR MEMORIAL

Antonia Reeve

This image shows the main classically styled hall of the memorial. Around the building hang the regimental colours of the units together with their insignia carved into the stonework. The red leather binders hold the Rolls of Honour for individual regiments and units. Around the top of the wall, just below the barrel-vaulted ceiling, can be seen the names of some of the battles in which Scottish forces were involved during the First World War, including the Somme, the Marne and the Aisne. To the left of this image is a plaque commemorating Field Marshal Douglas Haig, the commander-in-chief of the British forces for much of the war.

In 1917 discussions began to plan and create a national memorial to all of Scotland's war dead on land, in the air or at sea. What at first seemed to be an obvious and straightforward idea proved to be a long and drawn out process of compromise and change. The architect chosen was Sir Robert Lorimer but his original design was criticised by the Ancient Monuments Board (a government advisory body) and by other organisations including the Cockburn Association for its overwhelming impact on the historic stronghold of Edinburgh Castle. Others criticised the scheme for glorifying militarism. After years of discussion, a modified scheme on a smaller scale was eventually approved in 1923 and the new memorial opened in 1927. Located on the northern side of Crown Square at the very top of the rock on which Edinburgh Castle stands, the Scottish National War Memorial was constructed in a former barrack block with parts of its structure forming the memorial's exterior walls. It was paid for by public subscription and 200 of Scotland's most skilled artists and craftsmen produced elaborate sculptures, stained glass and carvings for the building. The design of the building was created to be spiritual without being specifically connected to any individual religion, to reflect the range of religious and secular groups who took part in the war. The main hall of the memorial is a room in classical style with a high barrel-vaulted ceiling. Inscribed around the walls are the names of the battles of the First World War in which Scottish forces fought and died. Elaborate stained glass windows light the hall and regimental and naval colours hang from the walls, with the regimental rolls of honour laid out in books around the building. At the heart of the memorial is the Gothic shrine. Here a steel casket, which contains the rolls of honour of all the Scots casualties of the First World War, rests on a marble plinth. Set into the bedrock of the castle and therefore by association into Scotland itself, the casket and its plinth link those buried and missing in distant places back to the land from which they came. Around the wall of the shrine is a bronze frieze depicting in detail every unit that served in

the war. Overhead an enormous oak sculpture of the Archangel Michael looks down, representing victory over war rather than victory in war, and the lasting peace that it was hoped the First World War would bring, and the same message is represented in the stained glass windows around the shrine. Sadly another 50,000 names would be added to the casket after the Second World War and new names continue to be added today.

THE SCOTTISH NATIONAL WAR MEMORIAL AS IT IS TODAY
Antonia Reeve

FUNDING THE NATIONAL MEMORIAL
National Museums of Scotland, licensor SCRAN

Postage stamps were issued to raise funds for the Scottish National War Memorial. This sheet of stamps commemorates Scots who served in the naval services. Other sheets were produced to commemorate Scottish regiments, women's services, the Royal Air Force and other troops.

THE MEMORIAL UNDER CONSTRUCTION, SUMMER 1924
RCAHMS

The memorial itself was built on the site of a former barrack block of the castle, and large parts of the existing building were used in its construction.

Epilogue

CHARLES HAMILTON SORLEY
Unknown photographer

While serving as a lieutenant in the Suffolk Regiment, Charles Hamilton Sorley took part in the battle of Loos in autumn 1915. On 13 October he was killed when he was shot in the head by a German sniper. His body was never recovered.

More than a century on from the world-changing events of the First World War, it can be difficult to comprehend the scale and impact of the conflict both at home and abroad. It is easy to see the war only through the fields of gravestones in the cemeteries of the Western Front and in the names inscribed on memorials. But, the war was much more than this. In effect, the world had been torn apart and the life people had known had been brought to an abrupt and violent end. The political and social changes that began during the war would continue across Scotland. Tanks built to fight on the Western Front were deployed in George Square in Glasgow within weeks of the end of fighting in January 1919 because of fears of a Russian-style socialist revolution in the city. Calls for the rights of workers to be protected and for women to be treated equally continued to grow. Medical breakthroughs such as artificial limbs, plastic surgery and psychological treatment all advanced by the war helped improve the lives of many thousands of individuals in the years afterwards. Friendships and romances forged in factories and hospitals proved as lasting as those between comrades in the trenches. The darker legacy of the war was that just twenty years later it led to an even deadlier conflict, and that it still influences the world as we know it today.

With the deaths of the last surviving men and women who took part in the First World War, the war has changed from a personal experience into one held in the pages of history books. We are fortunate that so many people who lived through the war shared their memories and experiences in stories, poems, diaries and letters home to loved ones. Documents, together with photographs, sketches and paintings, stand as witness to the part their authors played in one of the worst conflicts in human history. In addition to the personal testaments there stands the physical remains of the war across Scotland and the rest of Europe. While the surviving sites are quiet and lonely today, a century ago they were hives of activity and effort. These are the places where men and women joined the war effort, where they trained and from where they travelled to serve abroad. These are also the places where Scottish citizens stood up for their rights against those who would exploit them; the sites where they served to defend the country against the enemy; and where doctors and nurses worked to heal the shattered bodies and minds of wounded soldiers. And they are the places where some of them still remain, never to see the peace for which they fought.

Perhaps the final word on the war, and the importance of those places where countless thousands played a part, should go to one of those Scots who did so. Charles Hamilton Sorley was born in Aberdeen in 1895 and was studying in Germany when the war began. As a lieutenant in the Suffolk Regiment, he arrived in France in May 1915, and had been promoted to captain by August. A few weeks later, he would take part in the Battle of Loos. On 13 October 1915, Sorley was killed when he was shot in the head by a German sniper. His body was never recovered.

Sorley's poems were found in his kit bag after his death, and were first published in January 1916, meeting with immediate acclaim, and he is considered one of the finest of the First World War poets. His final poem, *When You See Millions of the Mouthless Dead* is a powerful indication of the scale of the slaughter on the front lines. But it is a single stanza in another poem, *Barbury Camp*, that reminds us why these now silent places are important. It describes his own experience, and reflects the experiences of millions of others from across the globe who found their world transformed by the events in which they took part, and the places where they witnessed them.

And here we strove, and here we felt each vein,
Ice-bound, each limb fast-frozen, all night long.
And here we held communion with the rain
That lashed us into manhood with its thong,
Cleansing through pain.
And the wind visited us and made us strong.

Glossary

EVER VIGILANT
RCAHMS

This coast artillery emplacement, at Vementry in Shetland, still has both of its First World War 6 inch guns in place, with their thick armour plating to protect the crew.

AIRSHIP
Airships were one of the major forms of flight around the time of the First World War, used for both commercial and military purposes. They came in both rigid and non-rigid types, with rigid airships using a metal frame to support their shape, while the kite balloons mentioned below were a type of non-rigid example. The term Zeppelin is often used to describe any rigid airship, particularly those used by the Germans, although this actually refers only to the airships manufactured by the German company Luftschiffbau Zeppelin. Airships were used by both sides in the conflict, providing long-range reconnaissance and offensive capabilities, which were not possible with early aeroplanes, although they would be surpassed by them before the end of the war.

ANTI-SUBMARINE BOOM
A large steel mesh net designed to prevent submarines entering a harbour in secret. The net would hang from floats on the surface and, where possible, would be fixed to anchor points on the bottom. In relatively shallow water (such as parts of the Forth) the nets would be slung between 'dolphins', which were, heavy timber pillars set on the seabed. Parts of the boom could be opened to allow access (usually a naval trawler opened and closed the gate). Light booms were slung between naval trawlers and could be moved around to provide protection for the fleet when it was exercising in the outer part of the Forth estuary, beyond the protection of the fixed booms and coast guns.

BLOCKSHIPS
Obsolete ships, which were purposefully sunk in order to block or restrict access to shipping through a particular area of shallow water.

CALIBRE
The internal diameter of a gun barrel, also often used to describe the gun and its ammunition in the case of artillery. In general, larger calibre artillery guns had higher range and more destructive power. Some guns were described by the weight of their shell (for example 12 pounder).

CHAIN OF EVACUATION
The term used to describe the process by which wounded soldiers were evacuated from the front line to an area where they could receive appropriate treatment and recovery time.

DEFENCE ELECTRIC LIGHT
A DEL was an electric searchlight that assisted gun batteries in finding targets at night. Depending on which was more effective for a particular location, DELs would be fitted with either a fixed or movable searchlight beam.

GOTHA BOMBER
The Gotha G.V bomber was one of Germany's most common heavy bomber aircraft during the First World War. They had an exceptionally long range for the time, and were used to attack the south east of England, as well as the allied front lines. Scotland was outside of the bomber's range.

INDICATOR NETS
These nets, similar to an anti-submarine boom, hung from surface buoys and covered the access to an anchorage estuary. They were much lighter than the anti-submarine booms and were purposefully designed to enable sections to break when hit by submarines, causing the submarine to drag a section of net with it. When the net was broken, lights would be activated on the net's surface edge. This enabled defending vessels to track and attack the submerged enemy vessel. These defences were used particularly on the Firth of Forth.

KITE BALLOON
A small airship balloon that could be connected to a cable attached to a ship or an anchor point on the ground. Beneath it hung a woven basket to accommodate two or three observers. The balloons could be winched out as needed to provide a heightened observation platform to watch for enemy shipping.

NEW ARMY
The term used to describe the vast number of new units raised from volunteers and later from conscripts to provide the additional manpower that Lord Kitchener believed would be required to conduct the war. Kitchener persuaded the government to authorise these new units because he had doubts about the effectiveness of the Territorial units, and feared (erroneously as it turned out) that few Territorials would volunteer to fight abroad.

PILLBOXES AND BLOCKHOUSES
Reinforced structures, which provided defensive strong points for infantry. Pillboxes were most often built of concrete or brick. They were much in evidence on the landward side of the coast batteries on the Clyde. Blockhouses were protected by raised earth banks round them. Blockhouses often had beds and cooking facilities, to allow a permanent resident garrison. They were used around the coast batteries on the Forth and were constructed from a range of material, although concrete was most commonly used.

QF GUN – QUICK FIRING GUN
The QF gun was an artillery gun designed to fire multiple rounds in quick succession, to engage fast-moving targets more effectively. It could fire at speed because the explosive charge (the shell) and the charge that propelled the shell out of the barrel were packed together in a brass case; larger guns had separate shells and charges, the latter being packed in cloth bags.

ROYAL ARMY MEDICAL CORPS
The RAMC was the branch of the military tasked with medical care both at the front lines and at home. A sixth of the civilian medical profession in Scotland had volunteered to serve in the RAMC by February 1915.

ROYAL GARRISON ARTILLERY
This was part of the Royal Artillery, in Scotland the RGA was largely made up of volunteer units assigned to man coast artillery guns. The RGA also became responsible for the very large number of heavy artillery pieces deployed on the Western Front. The coast batteries on the Sutors, defending the naval base at Cromarty, were manned by naval and Royal Marine personnel; the Scapa Flow guns were manned by RGA and naval personnel.

TERRITORIAL AND VOLUNTEER UNITS
In 1908 the former volunteer units were absorbed into a larger and more efficient territorial army, which provided a reserve force of part-time infantry (within the existing regimental structure), cavalry (in separate 'Yeomanry' units), such as the Fife & Forfar or Ayrshire Yeomanry, Royal Artillery, and supply and medical units.

Further Reading and Online Resources

FURTHER READING

Malcolm Brown and Patricia Meehan, *Scapa Flow: The Reminiscences Of Men And Women Who Served In Scapa Flow In The Two World Wars*, Stroud, 2008

William F. Hendrie, *The Forth at War*, Edinburgh, 2002

Wiiliam F. Hendrie and Donald Macleod, *The Bangour Story: A History of Bangour Village and General Hospitals*, Aberdeen, 1991

James Miller, *Scapa*, Edinburgh, 2005

Brian D. Osborne and Ronald Armstrong, *Glasgow: A City at War*, Edinburgh, 2003

Brian D. Osborne and Ronald Armstrong, *The Clyde at War*, Edinburgh, 2005

Trevor Royle, *The Flowers of the Forest: Scotland and the First World War*, Edinburgh, 2007

Geoffrey Stell, *Orkney at War: Defending Scapa Flow Volume 1: World War 1*, Kirkwall, 2011

ONLINE RESOURCES

Resources particularly relevant to the First World War in Scotland

Dr Gordon J. Barclay, *The Built Heritage of the First World War*, 2014; available online at http://www.historic-scotland.gov.uk/built-heritage-ww1.pdf or http://www.rcahms.gov.uk/rcahms_media/files/publications/built_heritage_ww1_29nov2013.pdf

Edinburgh's War: http://www.edinburghs-war.ed.ac.uk/

First World War.com website: http://firstworldwar.com/

The First World War Centenary: http://www.1914.org

The Home Front Legacy project: http://www.homefrontlegacy.org.uk

Remembering Scotland at War: http://www.rememberingscotlandatwar.org.uk/

Scapa Flow Landscape Partnership: http://www.scapaflow.co/

Scapa Flow Visitor Centre & Museum: http://www.scapaflow.co.uk/sfvc.htm

The Scottish War Memorials Project: http://warmemscot.s4.bizhat.com/

Stobs Military Camp website: http://stobs-camp.bizhat.com/

OTHER SOURCES

Canmore: http://canmore.rcahms.gov.uk/

Historic Scotland: http://www.historic-scotland.gov.uk/

Imperial War Museum: http://www.iwm.org.uk/

National Archives: http://www.nationalarchives.gov.uk/

National Army Museum: http://www.nam.ac.uk/

National Library of Scotland: http://www.nls.uk/

National Museum of Flight: http://www.nms.ac.uk/our_museums/museum_of_flight.aspx

National Records of Scotland: http://www.nrscotland.gov.uk/

National War Museum: http://www.nms.ac.uk/our_museums/war_museum.aspx

RCAHMS: http://www.rcahms.gov.uk/

Scottish National War Memorial: http://www.snwm.org/

HISTORIC SCOTLAND

Historic Scotland is responsible for safe-guarding the nation's historic environment and promoting its understanding and enjoyment. Many of the sites referred to in this book are recognised and protected through designation (either as scheduled monuments, listed buildings or as part of an Historic Marine Protected Area).

To find out more about these designations and the work of Historic Scotland visit:

www.historic-scotland.gov.uk

Army Structure

ARMY

An 'Army' would be made up of a number of Corps. There were several British 'Armies' on the Western Front, for example.

CORPS

In 1915–1917, a 'Corps' was made up of three Infantry Divisions, along with other resources under the direct control of the Corps commander. On the Western Front in 1916, for example, this included heavy artillery, transport, Royal Engineers (including 'mining' companies), Signals and mounted troops.

DIVISION

The Division, of which Infantry Divisions were the vast majority, was the smallest force which could operate as an independent unit in combat, with most having three Brigades of infantry along with artillery support.

BRIGADE

A Brigade consisted of between three and five battalions of infantry, although most had four battalions during the First World War. The Brigade could also include other arms, such as a Brigade machine-gun Company. Brigades were often a similar sized formation to a peacetime Regiment. In most Brigades the Battalions would not all be drawn from the same Regiment. For example, the 1st Brigade of the 1st Division at the Battle of the Somme in 1916 comprised two 'Regular' Battalions – 1st Battalion Black Watch and 1st Battalion Cameron Highlanders – and two of Kitchener's 'New Army Battalions – 10th Battalion Gloucester Regiment and 8th Battalion Royal Berkshires. On the occasions where multiple Battalions of one regiment were placed in the same Brigade, the casualty rates during battle could have a devastating impact on the Regiment's home community.

BATTALION

An infantry battalion had an establishment of around 1,000 men commanded by a Lieutenant-Colonel, with a Major as second-in-command. Prior to the war, each Scottish regiment had two 'regular' (that is full-time professional) battalions, 1st Battalion and 2nd Battalion. One of these would be stationed in the UK and the other on garrison duty around the British Empire at any one time. In addition to this, one or more volunteer regiments of Territorials were also connected to the regiment (3rd Battalion, 4th Battalion, 5th Battalion) and Kitchener's New Army recruits would also be attached to existing regiments as they were created, taking the next number in sequence.

COMPANY

Each battalion had four companies, each of about 250 men, named 'A' to 'D', usually commanded by a Major (or more often by a Captain as the war progressed). Even the most junior officers (2nd Lieutenants) were expected to be able to take over their Company if the senior officers were killed or injured.

PLATOON

Each Company had four Platoons of around sixty men, usually commanded by a 2nd Lieutenant. The Platoons of a Battalion were numbered one to sixteen.

Copyright and Photographic Credits

The publisher gratefully acknowledges the following individuals and organisations who have contributed photographic material to this book. Unless stated below, all images reproduced in this book are © Crown Copyright Historic Scotland.

Images: pages 58–9 and page 61 © Getty Images; page 51 reproduced by kind permission of GUARD Archaeology Ltd; page 95 © Nick Haynes; pages 66–7 © Andrew Lee; page 89 by kind permission of Ian Lowes Private Collection; page 81 courtesy of Edinburgh Napier University; pages 24, 27 and 40 © the National Archives; page 88 reproduced by kind permission of the Trustees of the National Library of Scotland; pages 28 and 54 © the Trustees of the National Museums of Scotland; page 80 © National Portrait Gallery, London; pages 14 and 32 Ordnance Survey Data © Crown Copyright and database right (2014); pages 98–9 and page 100 © Antonia Reeve; page 16 reproduced by kind permission of Scapa Flow Landscape Partnership; page 96 reproduced by kind permission of ScapaMAP; pages 44–5 (A0040) © Shetland Museum and Archives; page 37 reproduced by kind permission of the Turnberry Resort; and front cover © Spencer Woodcock

In addition, three agencies provided invaluable support to the project: the Imperial War Museum, the Royal Commission on the Ancient and Historical Monuments of Scotland and SCRAN. The images they supplied are as follows:

Imperial War Museum

Images: page 17 (SP 1053); page 18 and frontispiece (ART 991); page 21 (HU 66128); page 26 (ART 1384); page 27 (Q 115130); page 29 (Q 115131G); pages 30–31 (Q 80597); page 35 (Q 44211); page 36 (SP 365); page 55 (Q 18775); pages 62–3 (D 19391); pages 84–5 (Q 56594); page 89 (HU 75099); page 35 (Q 44210); and page 96 (SP 1626). All images are © Imperial War Museum

RCAHMS (www.rcahms.gov.uk)

Images: cover image (DP 006188) © Crown Copyright; page 11 (SC 1403508) © courtesy of RCAHMS; page 12 and back cover (DP 042230) © Crown Copyright; page 17 (SC 910816) © courtesy of RCAHMS; page 41 (DP 058347) © RCAHMS (Aerial Photography Collection); page 47 (SC 684599) © Crown Copyright; page 48 (DP 033071) © Crown Copyright; page 49 (DP 084318) © Crown Copyright; page 50 (DP 066642) © RCAHMS (Aerial Photography Collection); page 52 (SC 1257505) © RCAHMS (Aerofilms Collection); page 53 (DP 045364) © RCAHMS (Aerial Photography Collection); page 57 (SC 645637) © RCAHMS; page 65 (SC 1256881) © RCAHMS (Aerofilms Collection); page 68 (DP 102778) © Crown Copyright; page 74 (DP 028504) and (DP 028469) © Crown Copyright; pages 86–7 (DP 026878) © RCAHMS (Aerial Photography Collection); page 95 (SC 684406) © Crown Copyright; page 101 (SC 708451) © Crown Copyright; and page 104 (SC 444408) © Crown Copyright.

SCRAN (www.scran.co.uk)

Images: page 6 (000-000-033-824-R) © Glasgow City Council; pages 8–9 (000-000-182-903-R) © Orkney Islands Council; page 19 (000-000-097-330-R) © Richard Welsby; page 20 (000-000-182-829-R) © Orkney Islands Council; page 21 (000-000-182-702-R) © Orkney Islands Council; page 25 (000-000-602-118-R) © Scottish Life Archive; page 29 (000-000-586-770-R) © The Scotsman Publications Ltd; page 33 (000-000-129-428-R) © Courtesy of the Bruce/Leslie Collection; page 33 (000-000-496-177-R) © Montrose Air Station Museum Trust; page 34 (000-000-487-210-R) © Museum of Flight, National Museums of Scotland; page 37 (000-000-128-734-R) © Museum of Flight, National Museums of Scotland; page 51 (000-000-163-162-R) © West of Scotland Archaeology Service; page 56 (000-000-496-083-R) © Dugald Cameron; page 61 (000-000-537-406-R) © The Scotsman Publications Ltd; page 68 (000-000-129-524-R) © Courtesy of the Bruce/Leslie Collection; page 69 top (000-000-465-496-R) © National Museums Scotland; page 69 bottom (000-000-464-838-R) © National Museums Scotland; page 70 (000-000-033-828-R) © Glasgow City Council; pages 72–3 (000-000-033-831-R) © Glasgow City Council; page 75 (000-000-664-701-R) © Robert Gordon University; page 75 (000-000-093-043-R) © Lothian Health Services Archive; page 76 (000-000-463-449-R) © National Museums Scotland; page 76 (000-000-502-839-R) © British Red Cross, Mid and East Lothian Branch; pages 78–9 (000-000-599-741-R) © The Owen Estate; pages 82–3 (000-000-032-252-R) © British Geological Survey / NERC; pages 90–1 (000-000-182-894-R) © Orkney Islands Council; page 93 (000-000-099-981-R) © Glasgow Museums; page 93 (000-000-465-005-R) © National Museums Scotland; page 97 (000-000-464-771-R) © National Museums Scotland; and page 100 (000-180-002-407-R) © National Museums Scotland.